# MASTERING MENTAL HEALTH 2-IN-1

OVERCOMING OVERTHINKING AND ANXIETY -
THE ULTIMATE GUIDE TO CALM YOUR MIND

## KIRK TEACHOUT

IV QUARTER PUBLISHING

contained within this document, including, but not limited to, errors, omissions, or inaccuracies.

# CONTENTS

## OVERCOMING OVERTHINKING

## OVERCOMING ANXIETY

# OVERCOMING OVERTHINKING

## THE COMPLETE GUIDE TO CALM YOUR MIND BY CONQUERING ANXIETY, SLEEPLESSNESS, INDECISION, AND NEGATIVE THOUGHTS

# INTRODUCTION

*"You don't have to see the whole staircase, just take the first step."*

— MARTIN LUTHER KING, JR.

A few months after we had our second child, my wife, Lauren started looking for a new job. Unfortunately, everyone she interviewed with was looking to hire someone in the future. They were talking with possible prospects rather than hiring someone for an immediate position.

At the same time, I was watching our 1-year-old and our newborn while trying to run my business from home, but my business was not doing as well as it was before. During all of this, bills were coming in, our savings were dwindling, credit card debts were increasing, and I couldn't sleep. Lauren spent 7 weeks looking for an open position with nothing to show for it. This was when we went into panic mode. Throughout this process, we put our house up for sale, and the closing date was approaching the following week. Lauren and I were scrambling, trying to think, think, think — but we couldn't seem to grasp a solution. Between sleeplessness from raising a newborn, rising debt, and selling our house — with seemingly no end to the madness in sight — we were ready to give up.

Lauren had one final interview the week before our house was set to close, and it was 5 hours away. It seemed very promising, and we were hopeful. After meeting with the business again, the recruiter told Lauren that they were looking to possibly fill this position in the future. That long, silent, 5-hour drive home was defeating. It was depressing. It was one of the hardest times we have ever faced in our marriage.

This difficult time seeded thoughts of worry, anxiety, and the fear of not being good enough in my wife. She couldn't help but spiral into a cycle of overthinking. Were the positions with these companies truly not there yet, or was she not the right candidate for these jobs? Once these thoughts started to grow, they overflowed into other areas of our life. It put a strain on our marriage, and she started to question whether she was in the right industry to begin with.

"What if I'm stuck like this forever?" She would say, in her head, while lying in bed. "What if I'm incapable of being happy?" Little did she know, these nagging "what ifs" were one of the main things holding her back from achieving her goals and finding happiness in her life. Being a devoted husband to an overthinker got me overthinking a few things myself. Whenever we tried to have a conversation about her worries and anxiety, I felt paralyzed, not knowing how to answer. "How can I best support her?" I asked myself on several occasions. I received plenty of advice that should have been a solution — at least on paper. But nothing helped.

Lauren and I sloppily maneuvered our way through all of the situations life threw at us during that time, taking much-needed comfort in each other for the most part. Still, it was hard being 28, broke, and unhappy. Maybe you're experiencing something similar right now, and you should know that you're not alone. It's not easy treading water for weeks, months, or even years. It gets tiresome trying to keep your head above the surface.

Your mid to late twenties are a transitional period. You're not a kid anymore. Perhaps you're done with school and are just now entering the working world. In this day in age, it feels like it's almost impossible to find a career that matches your particular skill set. This can be awfully discouraging for a lot of people, and many in this age bracket end up overthinking everything. For people like us, the smallest inconvenience can feel like a total mess.

When the Covid-19 pandemic hit in 2020, a large number of people fell on hard times. As a result of the pandemic, our business was mandated to shut down with no end in sight. We could not pay our team, let alone our monthly bills. All we could do was sit around and wait. This was something a lot of people faced during this time. It was scary and discouraging not knowing when it was going to end.

Some even had to move back in with their parents due to financial hardship. Moving back in with your parents when you are in your mid-twenties or older can be somewhat of a shock to your system. It's scarily easy to fall into depression, and some might even try to self-medicate with drugs and alcohol. Living out of your old childhood bedroom can make you feel like you cannot properly grow as an adult and as a person. When young adults don't have room to grow and thrive, they'll often start to feel very dissatisfied with their lives.

Even for those whose parents didn't mind taking them under their roof when the pandemic hit, this was still an incredibly difficult time. You've undoubtedly noticed the impact the pandemic had on your own life, on society, and on the world. Things will never go back to the way they were before, which is both a good thing and a bad thing in limitless ways.

People who are prone to overthinking don't like change. We thrive on routine, and those of us who are new to the working world are not necessarily used to making ends meet — particularly in a world where work culture has gotten incredibly callous. The world has changed significantly since your parents were your age; chances are, they probably don't understand what you're going through.

As a society, there are parts of us that are broken, and that's sad — but we're also strong because of it. Like your muscles, when you engage in excessive exercise, you need time to heal. When you do heal, you're bound to be ten times stronger after the fact. It's hard to grow up and become an adult. It's complicated, heartbreaking, and lovely all at the same time. Life simultaneously feels endless and fleeting, and I'm not sure what to do about it other than just take it one day at a time.

Your young adult years tend to be full of change — which can be wonderful — but it can also be awfully jarring. Not only are you changing personally and professionally, but you're also seeing your friends and loved ones at different stages of achievement than you. Maybe your best friend got married at 27 while you're still single at 30. Maybe your sister started her own business at 29 while you're actively pursuing your ideal career at 31. Everyone seems to be a contender in this invisible race, against themselves and others — not to mention the various versions of how people present themselves on social media. Like my wife was, you may be unhappy at work. Perhaps you've experienced thoughts like: "what am I even doing with my life," or "what if I'm stuck in this same position forever?"

Do you see what I mean? Overthinking is a cyclical and dangerous cycle. It makes you feel stuck (a concept known as "analysis paralysis") because you're creating these endless possible scenarios in your head, but at the same time, you don't know what to do to make these scenarios happen (or not happen, if your anxiety makes everything feel like a catastrophe).

This state of paralysis and fear can make you feel like you're unable to be your authentic self. You may feel like you're losing sight of who you truly are, and close yourself off from your loved ones. You might also experience a drop in energy because you're overexerting yourself by thinking too much. This can lead to loss of sleep and appetite, which means your physical and mental health could take a dive.

Does any of this sound familiar? If so, again, you're definitely not alone. I know this because I have been there. As has Lauren. We've been through our ups and downs, sometimes feeling like we couldn't pull ourselves out of this vicious cycle. Like so many others, we tried a lot of self-help books, but what really helped us was doing our own, detailed research.

We didn't focus on how to stop overthinking. We focused on identifying why we were overthinking. We spent months trying to find the root cause of our over-thinking and researched practical solutions to help us overcome it. It often felt like we took two steps forward and one step back, but that was still one step further from where we were before.

Breaking away from a chronic tendency to overthink takes time. After much research and practical applica-tion, Lauren and I have put this book together to help others like us: regular people, living regular lives in a world that seems to be speeding by.

Instead of jumping into a series of cookie-cutter suggestions on how to stop overthinking, let's spend some time understanding you. Let's delve into how you may be overthinking and why. Then, let's take a look at the solutions you come up with, and find those that work for you in your own unique way.

As you read, you'll see reflection questions throughout this book. Try to take a moment and really think about each question. How do these questions apply to your experiences in life? Reflecting on these things is a necessary part of overcoming overthinking, so give it your best shot!

# 1

# BRAIN PAIN

*"Overthinking, also best known as creating problems that are never there."*

— DAVID SIKHOSANA

When you're getting bombarded by an onslaught of disorganized, often self-deprecating thoughts, it can make it very difficult for you to focus on your work, get enough sleep, and generally live your life. You might find yourself wishing that your brain would just shut up for a few minutes. Those of us who are prone to overthinking certainly understand that sentiment!

Something Lauren and I learned while doing our

research is that before you overcome your overthinking, you've got to *understand* your overthinking. So, what is overthinking, exactly? Is there really such a thing as thinking too much? To put it simply, people who are plagued by overthinking often cannot stop themselves from dwelling on the same thought over and over again. They might spend too much of their time and energy over-analyzing certain situations.

For example, an overthinker might worry that they've left the stove on while out at a social gathering. The stove becomes all they can think about for the rest of the evening, whereas someone who doesn't overthink everything wouldn't worry about it too much. An over-thinker might experience thoughts like: "what if the house catches on fire?" or "what if my pets get carbon monoxide poisoning?" Needless to say, these types of thoughts are more harmful than they are helpful.

It can be difficult to identify the difference between helpful and harmful thoughts. Most overthinkers have both, but they may be so intertwined with each other that it's hard to tell which thoughts are actually helpful among the onslaught of harmful thoughts. If you're worried you left your stove on, "what if my house catches on fire," is a harmful thought because the likeli-hood of that happening is incredibly small. A helpful thought, in this scenario, might be: "I always turn the stove off, so there's nothing to stress about." Dissecting these thoughts and differentiating between them can be quite helpful!

*Reflection question: are the majority of my thoughts helping or harming me?*

There are two types of overthinking, namely rumination and worrying. Rumination is cyclical and involves rehashing events that caused you pain or emotional turmoil in the past. Let's say you had a toxic friendship in high school, and this person made you feel like you were the problem. Even if you've grown up and realized they were the toxic one, you might still lie awake at night wondering what exactly you did wrong — even if you did absolutely nothing wrong!

Excessive worrying is slightly more common and typically involves hyper-focusing on something that's going to happen in the future. Maybe, for example, you've got a big presentation at work next week. You might start imagining every possible thing that could go wrong (i.e. "what if I get stage fright?" or "what if that one male coworker talks over me again?"). Someone who overthinks these things will have a hard time not feeling like a nervous wreck. Some might even panic and jump ship. They might think, "I can't do this," and avoid the responsibility altogether because they're stuck in a state of analysis paralysis.

Ruminating and obsessing over the things you can't control can cause what we call "brain pain." Basically, your brain gets so exhausted from overthinking that it gets stuck in that polarizing state of fear. You might find yourself breaking down more often than usual (i.e. getting overwhelmed by the smallest inconveniences). You might feel like your brain isn't functioning as it should because it's so overworked.

It's also important to keep in mind that overthinking is oftentimes a symptom of anxiety and depression. Anxiety and depression go hand-in-hand most of the time. Your overthinking tendencies may be a result of your anxiety, which then might trigger thoughts of worthlessness (depression). Attending weekly therapy and taking medication can sometimes help over-thinkers, but that's a bandaid, not a cure. Everyone is different, though, and it's definitely worth looking into — especially if you know you suffer from anxiety and/or depression.

*Reflection question: How many signs of overthinking am I displaying in my life?*

In order to gain a deeper understanding of your overthinking tendencies, it can be helpful to know the signs. Everyone worries sometimes, but it can be diffi-cult to identify when your worrying has become a real problem. You should know that people who don't overthink things won't spend hours or even weeks stressing about a problem they have no control over. They're able to say: "well, there's nothing I can do about that right now," and simply go on with their lives.

This can be rather confusing for overthinkers. We can say mantras in our heads like "there's nothing I can do about that right now, and that's okay," or "this is not worth stressing about," but our brains won't stop nagging us. It can get to a point where the thoughts you're getting bombarded with are intrusive. You don't want to think these things; you just do!

So, the question becomes: how can I get rid of these thoughts? How can I prevent them from controlling my life? If you're going to reduce your overthinking tendencies, you're going to want to be able to identify the signs that indicate you're overthinking. For example, if you find yourself having a lot of negative thoughts or obsessing over things outside of your control, you're probably overthinking.

If you constantly feel anxious about something — and seem unable to think about anything else — that's a good indication that your overthinking has become a problem. You might feel mentally exhausted, or have a hard time relaxing even when nothing particularly stressful is happening in the moment. You might find yourself seeking reassurance from others, or being short or irritable with your loved ones.

Overthinkers always jump to the worst-case scenario, even if that scenario is not particularly logical.

Think back to the example of worrying that you left your stove on and therefore your house might catch on fire. When you explain your thought process to someone, they might point out that the way you're thinking doesn't really make sense — which you'll know is true — but you won't be able to stop overthinking anyway. You'll second-guess yourself, and have trouble concentrating at work. You'll feel on edge and replay situations in your head, knowing full well that that type of thinking isn't productive.

## The Neuroscience of Overthinking

One of the best ways to understand overthinking is to understand the science behind it. Science rules, after all! Constant thinking is supposed to lead to problem-solving, but not all problems are easily solved just by thinking about them. When our problems are too complicated, we can get stuck in that paralyzing loop of overthinking. Although your energy is being drained from thinking too much, you're not making any progress, which can be incredibly discouraging.

Your brain is complicated, and like most issues that stem from mental illness, overthinking is largely chemical. You may not be aware of it, but when you engage in overthinking, the chemicals in your brain go into hyperdrive. These chemicals — namely dopamine, serotonin, adrenaline, and cortisol — react with one another in different and complex ways. This is where things get a bit complicated, so let's go over what each of these chemicals does in a bit more detail.

## Dopamine

Dopamine plays a major role in your brain's functioning. If you've ever felt exceptionally happy after exercising or playing with your dog, for example, that's dopamine in action! Dopamine is very much connected to your brain's reward center. When you do something nice for yourself, dopamine gets released, and you feel a sense of satisfaction and pleasure.

A lot of people think of dopamine as "what makes you happy," but it also plays a role in regulating your emotions and driving your various motivations. People with proper dopamine levels might have an easier time focusing and staying motivated than those who are lacking dopamine. Overthinkers, for example, tend to lack dopamine, which can heavily contribute to that lethargic feeling you've probably grown accustomed to.

## Serotonin

It's easy to confuse serotonin for dopamine. Both are happy emotion regulators, and upon release into your brain, serotonin and dopamine can make you feel like a million bucks. Serotonin, however, is much like a conductor. You have a symphony of neurotransmitters firing in your brain at all times, and serotonin is responsible for making sure things don't go haywire.

Serotonin plays a huge role in mood regulation, the way you compose yourself in certain situations, and your overall sense of well-being. If you feel calm and collected after going for a walk or drinking a nice cup of tea, for example, it's because these activities release serotonin. Having enough serotonin in your system is also crucial when it comes to maintaining a regular sleep schedule and a healthy appetite.

## Adrenaline

People don't go bungy-jumping because it's pleasant and calming; they do it for the adrenaline rush. When you overcome a particular obstacle or do something you would never have dreamed of doing years ago, adrenaline gets released into your brain. Adrenaline is a very powerful thing. A mother whose infant has gotten trapped underneath a car, for example, will be able to lift the car up off of her child in order to save them — thanks to pure adrenaline!

Adrenaline also plays a role in properly regulating your blood pressure and heart rate. It's what helps you focus and overcome challenges that seem impossible. When the going gets tough, adrenaline is what gives you the energy and sometimes superhuman strength you need to accomplish anything. It can be an absolute godsend for overthinkers.

### Cortisol

Cortisol is meant to be a guardian angel of sorts. It's responsible for regulating the way your body responds to stressful situations. When you're faced with something stressful or scary, cortisol gets released. This causes your blood vessels to constrict and your heart rate to increase, which prepares your body for whatever is about to happen next.

The problem with cortisol, though, is it can have negative effects on your brain and body if too much of it gets released. If you're constantly stressed, for example — like most overthinkers are — your body is going to get overloaded with cortisol. This is what causes symptoms like panic attacks, mood swings, and rumination. Not fun.

*Reflection question: What might be at the root of my overthinking?*

## Why Do We Do It?

Asking "why do I overthink everything" might feel like you're overthinking your overthinking, but I promise — asking yourself this question is a necessary part of overcoming overthinking! People commonly overthink when attempting to solve their problems or make an important decision, not knowing that overthinking can actually cloud their judgment and negatively affect their decision-making process.

Overthinking can be habitual as well. A lot of people with severe overthinking tendencies have grown accustomed to using overthinking as a coping mechanism. It was the only way they knew how to deal with whatever challenging experiences they went through while growing up. Overthinking, then, can often be a trauma response. For example, if your mom had trouble finding work when you were a kid — and this heavily affected the well-being of your family — you might start overthinking every time a job interview doesn't pan out the way you wanted it to. This might be especially true if you're raising a family of your own! Generational trauma is very real, and as a young adult, you might have a tendency to not want to go through the same struggles your parents did.

At this point, you might be wondering: "well, I haven't experienced any significant trauma in my life, so why am I overthinking everything?" This is a good question, and to put it simply, excessive overthinking isn't always rooted in trauma. Many people develop overthinking tendencies later in life in response to a particularly stressful event. If you constantly feel stressed at work, this can also contribute to your over-thinking habit. You might feel helpless at work or in other areas of your life, and overthinking can make you feel like you have some semblance of control.

A lot of overthinkers are perfectionists who fear failure — which is not in and of itself a bad thing — but if you can't reign it in a bit, you'll probably end up leading a pretty stressful life. Overthinking the prob-lems in your life can feel like a good way to distract yourself from the possibility that you might fail. Over-thinkers also tend to avoid conflict at all costs, which is mentally exhausting. Fear of conflict is again rooted in anxiety, so it's not something you want to ignore.

Furthermore, overthinking has some short-term, dopamine-boosting side effects that some people can subconsciously get addicted to. The people in their lives may express pity or sympathy for them, which, let's be honest, feels *good*. People also often overthink impor-tant decisions because they don't want to make these decisions in the first place, and I get that! It can feel like a lot of pressure.

It's also important to keep in mind that overthinking

can be a symptom of OCD (Obsessive Compulsive Disorder). In fact, OCD is oftentimes the underlying cause of intrusive thoughts. If you truly feel like you can't stop your thoughts, and they're coming at you a million miles a minute, it might be a good idea to make an appointment with a psychiatrist.

## How Much Thinking is Too Much?

Healthy thinking is all about balance, and admittedly, this balance can be hard to find. Thinking too much can make you feel like you're stuck in an endless loop, which is not going to help you solve your problems or make any crucial decisions. Thinking is complicated, and everyone has a different way of thinking. I don't really have a solid answer to the question: "how much thinking is too much" because that's something you need to figure out for yourself.

When you catch yourself overthinking, it's important to be mindful and try to take a step back. Think to yourself: "are these thoughts helpful or harmful?" Once you're able to identify the line between useful thinking and overthinking, you'll have a much easier time making sense of the issues you're facing in your life.

I will say that if your thinking is taking over every aspect of your life, you're probably thinking too much. If your overthinking leaves you feeling too paralyzed to do things like go to the grocery store or take care of yourself, then that's definitely an issue that needs to be addressed. If worrying about one thing leads to worrying about a number of other things, that's also an indication that you're thinking too much.

For example, if you're worried about whether or not you can afford to get takeout, you might then start worrying if you'll be able to afford rent that month. This might, in turn, lead to worrying about your job (i.e. "what will I do if I lose my job?"), which might make you start thinking about your career as a whole and whether or not your current career is even right for you.

As you can see, it's a vicious cycle. Most people don't even realize they're overthinking when they're doing it. It's hard to notice yourself overthinking when you're so caught up in, well... your thoughts. Thankfully, the more you learn to harness your overthinking, the more you'll be able to effectively reduce it!

**What is Overthinking Doing to You and Your Life?**

If you're an overthinker, it's time to reassess (but not overthink!) your life. By identifying the ways in which overthinking has impacted your life, you'll be able to start doing the work necessary to overcome it. Many people don't know this, but overthinking has physical effects as well as emotional effects. You can use the checklist below to evaluate your overthinking and get a better grasp on what you've been going through.

Keep in mind that you don't need to check off "severe" for every category listed below to be considered an overthinker. Some of the categories on this list might surprise you because it's not commonly known that symptoms like overeating skin disorders can be caused by overthinking. It makes sense the more you think about it, though. These symptoms (and many others on this list) are rooted in anxiety — which is a big reason people overthink.

RATE YOURSELF AS "MILD," "average," or "severe" for each category listed below:

Lack of focus:

- Mild
- Average
- Severe

Irritability:

- Mild
- Average
- Severe

Stress:

- Mild
- Average
- Severe

Anxiety:

- Mild
- Average
- Severe

INSOMNIA:

- Mild
- Average
- <u>Severe</u>

Undereating:

- Mild
- Average
- <u>Severe</u>

Overeating:

- <u>Mild</u>
- Average
- Severe

Racing thoughts:

- Mild
- Average
- <u>Severe</u>

GUT PAIN AND/OR digestive issues:

- Mild
- Average
- Severe

Hyperreactivity:

- Mild
- Average
- Severe

Indecision:

- Mild
- Average
- Severe

Procrastination:

- Mild
- Average
- Severe

ANALYSIS PARALYSIS:

- Mild
- Average
- Severe

Brain fog:

- Mild
- Average
- Severe

High blood pressure/chest pain/tachycardia:

- Mild
- Average
- Severe

Skin disorders — eczema, psoriasis, etc:

- Mild
- Average
- Severe

## INCREASED HEART RATE:

- Mild
- Average
- Severe

Dizziness:

- Mild
- Average
- Severe

Headaches:

- Mild
- Average
- Severe

Nausea:

- Mild
- Average
- Severe

FATIGUE:

- Mild
- <u>Average</u>
- Severe

Depression:

- Mild
- <u>Average</u>
- Severe

**Summary Box**

9/22 - Average
8/22 - Severe
5/22 - mild.

OVERCOMING overthinking won't be easy, but with the right tools on hand, it's absolutely possible. Remember: understanding your overthinking tendencies is a huge part of coping with and eventually overcoming them. Try talking to a therapist or journaling about where you think your overthinking stems from. By addressing the root cause of your overthinking habit, you'll be able to better understand and overcome it. Keep in mind, through it all, that overthinking affects millions of people all over the world. You're not alone, and you will get through this!

## Segue

Reducing your overthinking starts with analyzing what is actually going on inside your head. Learning to question those "what ifs" that seem a little bit outlandish can help you gain a better understanding of which thoughts are helpful and which thoughts are harmful. Working with your thoughts and analyzing them in a healthy way might sound like mental gymnastics, but it's all part of overcoming overthinking. See for yourself!

# 2

## IT BEGINS WITH A THOUGHT

*"Worrying is like a rocking chair. It gives you something to do, but it doesn't get you anywhere."*

— VAN WILDER

Thoughts are like a solar system. A vast expanse of never-ending stars. Some peter out over time and fade into nothingness. Some shine brighter than all the others and form constellations against the night sky — a network of thoughts, so to speak. Like stars, our thoughts are what guide us home when the world seems all too dark. What are we supposed to do, though, when our thoughts guide us in the wrong direction?

One of the most important things I've come to learn is that you are what you think, and perhaps even more so, you are what you do. Your thoughts are informed by your experiences — the good and the bad. They've formed into what they are today because of what you've been told by your parents, or taught by your teachers in school. As you get older, you learn how to think for yourself, and that becomes the foundation for who you are as a person.

Let's say, for example, that your parents told you all about their political views when you were a kid. Or, maybe, you just overheard them talking about it. It's natural for kids to mirror their parents, and that includes what they say, do, and think. Perhaps you went to school and talked at length about things you knew nothing about, simply because that's what you heard the adults around you conversing about.

Maybe someone told you that you were wrong — that the way you were thinking was *wrong* — and that made you feel bad inside. How, after all, could your parents be wrong? Perhaps you felt defensive at first, but later came to realize that your parents' way of thinking didn't actually sit right with you. Around the age of 12, your thinking gets more complex, which is why some people stop relying on the information their parents give them when they reach adolescence.

When you were in high school or college, you may

have started doing your own research and forming your own thoughts about things. You may have also started experiencing intrusive or unwanted thoughts around this age, which undoubtedly made things a bit more complicated. When you're in your twenties and thirties, it becomes your responsibility to figure out which thoughts are truly your own and which thoughts are doing more harm than good.

Taking your thoughts by the reigns isn't easy, but practice makes perfect. Being mindful and open to even the bad thoughts — letting them pass over you like water off a duck's back — is the key to being stoic and overcoming overthinking. A big part of being a mindful thinker and practicing stoicism is asking yourself where your thoughts are coming from in the first place.

*Reflection question: Where do my thoughts come from?*

The truth is, your thoughts determine your reality. They affect everything that you are and that you're going to be — your emotions, your choices, your actions, and even your physical state of being. This is why people with overthinking tendencies often feel like they're drowning. Their thoughts are often all over the place, misinformed, or fueled by mental illnesses like anxiety, depression, and OCD. Usually, if your thoughts are faulty or unclear, your actions will be misguided.

Thankfully, though, there are a few ways you can combat this. You see, your thoughts don't actually hold any real power over you. They're just thoughts! You don't have to ignore your bad thoughts, necessarily, but you also don't have to feed the fire. For example, let's say you're having a particularly bad day and your brain is telling you things like "you're worthless," or "you'll never amount to anything." If you engage with these thoughts, you're simply entertaining the mean voice in your head.

If you continue to engage with your harmful thoughts, it can significantly affect your well-being. Not only will you start to believe that these thoughts are true, but you'll also begin to feel bad physically. You might feel sick to your stomach, or emotionally fatigued. You might feel like you want to crawl into bed and not speak to anyone for the rest of the night. This is what I call "curling up to your depression." Wallowing in your negative thoughts might seem warm and inviting, but it's actually a weight on your chest that keeps you from living your life to the fullest.

At this point, maybe you're thinking something along the lines of: "yes, I know they're just thoughts, but thoughts are pretty powerful and I can't help feeling down on myself." This is very real, and I'm not here to tell you how to feel. Sometimes you really can't help what you feel. You can, however, help what you think if you're willing to put the necessary work in. Trust me. It's worth it.

One thing you can do to combat your negative thoughts is instead try to engage with your positive, self-empowering thoughts. Your negative thoughts might seem a lot louder than your positive thoughts, but it's sort of like that one guy who used to steal your lunch money and belittle you back in high school: he's just a bully, and you don't have to listen to him.

When your thoughts of worry and worthlessness are bringing you down, you've got to dig deep and consider all of the amazing parts of yourself. Yes, you had a bad day, but you did a really great job standing up for yourself at work and you should be proud of yourself for that. Yes, you fumbled a few orders at the restaurant you work at, but now that you're home, you can focus your time and energy on doing something you love.

When you get trapped in the cycle of overthinking, it's important to consider which thoughts are actually real. Remember, the human brain is incredibly complicated. Your synapses are firing all the time, and your actions are releasing chemicals that react with one another in strange ways. It's easy to feel like your thoughts are surrounding you from all sides, but you don't need to let them dogpile you. You're stronger than that.

*Reflection question: Are my thoughts always real or true?*

## Faulty Cognitive Biases

So, why in the world do we experience thoughts that aren't true? Why do we let these thoughts negatively impact us, even when we *know* they're not true? The answer is quite fascinating and surprisingly simple. All of us, in our everyday lives, are heavily under the influence of cognitive biases. Cognitive biases distort your thinking and influence your beliefs, so much so that many believe their cognitive biases to be the absolute truth.

In order to better understand how cognitive biases work — and how these biases affect your thinking — let's go over some of the most common types of cognitive biases people face in their daily lives below:

### The Confirmation Bias

It's undeniably human to want to be validated in your beliefs. Most people develop a confirmation bias because they only listen to or seek out information that confirms their own beliefs. Let's say, for example, that your uncle believes the earth is flat. Despite there being way more sources available that prove the earth is spherical, he's going to seek out the one or two sources that "prove" the earth is flat — simply because he has a confirmation bias.

People with a strong confirmation bias oftentimes won't be able to think logically about what they've already decided is true. If an overthinker truly believes they're worthless, they won't believe you when you tell them they're not. Some overthinkers might even participate in what is known as "digital self-harm," which involves going on chat forums and asking strangers to validate their thoughts and feelings of worthlessness.

## The Anchoring Bias

It's also human nature to believe that the first thing you think is what is truly "correct." No one likes admitting they're wrong, therefore, people who have a difficult time swallowing their pride might end up developing an anchoring bias. For example, a doctor who misdiagnoses a patient the first time they see them might refuse to consider other diagnoses when the same patient inevitably comes in again. It's an "I'm right, and that's final," kind of mindset.

People with overthinking tendencies may develop this particular bias when it comes to things like job searching. If they already have an idea in their head of what they want their career path to be, they might be unwilling to branch out and try something that would ultimately end up working better for them. They have already latched onto this "ideal career," and no other career can compare in their mind because they're influenced by a heavy anchoring bias.

## The Hindsight Bias

Have you ever had a conversation with a friend where you admitted something to them, and they said something along the lines of: "Ha! I knew it all along!" We love being able to "predict" things, don't we? The hindsight bias is what gets people into things like betting and gambling, despite the fact these things don't always work out in the gambler's favor.

The hindsight bias is a pretty common one, and it's particularly strong because logic can occasionally be used to back up some hindsight biases. The hindsight bias often goes hand-in-hand with the confirmation bias as well. Your uncle, who believes the world is flat, might be absolutely convinced that a certain political candidate is going to win an election because of the "evidence" they've seen online.

## The Misinformation Effect

MEMORY IS A FUNNY THING. Even if a particular memory seems crystal clear in your mind, it might not be entirely reliable or true to what actually happened. Research on the subject shows that memory is incredibly susceptible. Watching news coverage of an event you personally witnessed can skew your memory of what actually happened, for example. This, of course, would also skew your thought process regarding that particular event.

As much as we like to believe we can remember things perfectly well, most people's memories are flawed and full of gaps. This is totally normal, but it can, unfortunately, lead to people experiencing false beliefs and spreading misinformation based on those beliefs. Your brain doesn't particularly like memory gaps, so it will often fill them in with what it believes to be true.

## The False Consensus Effect

We like to believe that our friends and family members will always agree with us on everything no matter what. You can of course still love someone without fully agreeing with them on certain things, but it's always nice when people agree with you, don't you think? The false consensus effect occurs when people automatically believe that the people around them have the same values as they do.

According to research, this effect stems from people spending too much time with people who *do* have the same exact values as them — so much so that they start to believe the majority of the world's population thinks the same way they do. This bias can significantly impact your thinking, as you might not be able to see or understand things from other perspectives.

### The Halo Effect

First impressions are everything, but they aren't always correct. The halo effect is the tendency for people to have preconceived notions about a person based on their physical appearance. This is where the concept of "pretty privilege" comes from. Studies have shown that people are far more likely to believe and follow the ideas of someone who society considers physically attractive.

This cognitive bias can be particularly powerful. As unfair as it is, people who are perceived as more attractive are more likely to land jobs than those who are perceived as "average" or "unattractive." For people who overthink everything, not acing a job interview can lead them to believe that they're "too ugly" for that particular job. In reality, things aren't that black and white, but the halo effect does play a prominent role.

## The Self-Serving Bias

It's wonderful to succeed, but it's also okay to fail sometimes. Nobody's perfect, and a lot of overthinkers have a hard time accepting this. The self-service bias is essentially the tendency for people to praise themselves for their successes but blame their failures on things outside of their control. For example, when you do well on an exam at school, you'll be proud of yourself for working hard (as you should be.) If you don't do well on the exam, you might feel a bit disappointed in yourself, whereas someone with a self-serving bias will say: "I failed because other students were being too loud," or "I failed because the teacher didn't prepare us well enough."

## The Optimism Bias

There are certainly some people who are more pessimistic than optimistic, but most of us are honestly too optimistic for our own good. People with an optimism bias tend to believe that there's no way a negative life event — like divorce, for example — could possibly happen to them, despite the fact that divorce rates are constantly rising. Overthinkers with an optimism bias might go into a job interview so sure that they're going to get the job only to find out that the recruiter has already offered the job to someone else.

In this way, optimism can be dangerous. It can be difficult to find a healthy balance between optimism and pessimism, but it's a good idea to try to do so in order to save yourself some heartbreak and disappointment. Sometimes good things happen, and sometimes bad things happen. It's all just part of life. As you get older, though, things will get better. It's not too optimistic to think that!

## How Do We Combat Cognitive Biases?

Because cognitive biases are often something we experience subconsciously, it can be tricky to identify and appropriately address them. There are quite a few strategies you can use to reduce the extent to which your cognitive biases are affecting you, however. One thing that can help is being open to multiple perspectives from people with different backgrounds and experiences than your own. The world is vast, and there's more than one way to look at, well, everything! You might even discover something new about yourself.

It can also be helpful to be aware of some of the more common biases, such as the confirmation bias and the hindsight bias. If you catch yourself reacting to certain situations based on your biases, you'll be able to put a stop to them and think about the situation at hand with some clarity. This is a big part of practicing mindfulness as well. When you suspect your reacting to something based on a cognitive bias, take a step back and consider what might be influencing you to think in a certain way.

Another way people combat their cognitive biases is by taking lots of time to reflect. Consider journaling about your thoughts in order to make more sense of them, and again, remember to take other perspectives into account. It's also a good idea to try to seek out disconfirming evidence of what you believe is true. This will help you gain more knowledge of the subject, as well as not feed your confirmation bias.

It's also recommended that you practice your critical thinking skills. This involves questioning the validity of the evidence you would normally perceive as good enough "proof" of your opinions being "correct," and breaking down your own preconceived assumptions and judgments in order to make more accurate decisions about things. You should also try to keep in mind that challenging your cognitive biases takes time! It's not easy to always be aware of your own thoughts and biases, but the more you put the effort in, the more you'll notice a difference.

## Examining Your Thoughts

Most people don't know how much you can improve your life just by taking the time and space to examine your own thoughts. If you're familiar with Cognitive Behavioral Therapy, you've probably heard the phrase "inner critic" before. Everyone has a negative inner critic — a voice that basically amplifies your deepest insecurities. "You're worthless," the inner critic might say. "You're a hack. There's no way you'll get that job." Remember what I said earlier about the high school bully? *That's* your inner critic.

Observing your thoughts with mindfulness takes time and practice. We often think in negative patterns, which is how we get stuck in these seemingly endless cycles of overthinking. By identifying your negative thinking patterns and learning how to shift your unhelpful thoughts to the side (to make more room for your helpful ones!), you can dig yourself out of this vicious cycle.

*Reflection question: Can I control my thoughts?*

## Mastering Your Focus

A lot of people with overthinking tendencies don't know where to focus their attention. Your brain is saying, "hey, what if you don't ace that job interview?"

and "hey, what if you can't afford rent this month," and "hey, hey, hey —" Needless to say, it can be pretty relentless! If you're anything like Lauren and me, your negative thoughts have probably distracted you from completing various important tasks, like putting dinner on the table, or (if you're a student) getting your schoolwork done.

Thankfully, there are several helpful strategies you can use to strengthen your focus and improve your ability to concentrate on what's most important. For example, breaking your work down into smaller, more manageable chunks and prioritizing your tasks based on urgency can help you complete your work without getting overwhelmed by the amount of work you have to do.

It's also a good idea to eliminate distractions as much as you can. It's going to be pretty difficult to focus on the task at hand if you're attempting to scroll through Twitter and watch Youtube videos at the same time. I also recommend getting yourself a pair of noise-canceling headphones, as this can help a lot when it comes to reducing noisy distractions!

If you're working on something that you know is going to take a particularly long time, you can try out the Pomodoro Technique. This technique is super cool, and it honestly works wonders. The Pomodoro technique involves working on a task for about 25 minutes, then taking a short break so that you don't get burnt out. After four "pomodoros," you get to take an even longer break. Think of it as rewarding yourself with a break for getting 25 minutes of work done!

Naturally, it's also important to practice mindfulness throughout each day. Mindfulness techniques — like focusing on your breathing when you're feeling anxious or practicing mindful meditation — can be more helpful than you might think. Practicing mindfulness takes a lot of practice and time though, so don't feel frustrated if it doesn't help right away.

Finally, you should always take regular breaks during your work day. Moving your body is good for your brain, so taking a break to walk around or stretch every now and then is definitely a good idea. Going for a short walk or simply getting up from your chair for a few minutes is also a great way to clear your head if you feel yourself entering into a cycle of over-thinking.

**Interactive Element**

Recording and monitoring your thoughts is a big part of Cognitive Behavioral Therapy. When you experience a thought, try to write down how you reacted emotionally and practically after the fact. This is a great way to learn how to control and understand your thoughts, which is a crucial part of eventually overcoming your over-thinking tendencies.

**Summary Box**

UNDERSTANDING AND HARNESSING your thoughts takes a lot of time and practice, but it's certainly possible — especially when you have the right information and tools on hand. It's important to be mindful of your own cognitive biases, as these can severely skew your thinking. One way to be more aware of your cognitive biases is by taking the time to reflect on them. This might mean journaling or talking with a therapist about the biases you already know you have. Examining your thoughts every now and then by practicing mindfulness and removing distractions from your workspace is also a great way to combat cognitive biases and tighten the reigns on your thinking.

## Segue

What goes hand-in-hand with thoughts? Emotions, of course! Your thoughts are oftentimes what cause you to feel emotions like joy, sorrow, excitement, and anger. Those with overthinking tendencies often have a difficult time regulating their emotions, but don't worry! We'll talk about that next.

# 3

## THE STRESS CYCLE

*"Simple can be harder than complex: You have to work hard to get your thinking clean to make it simple. But it's worth it in the end because once you get there, you can move mountains."*

— STEVE JOBS

One of the most important things I've learned during this process is it can be difficult to separate your thoughts from your emotions. Both are complicated, and can seem nonsensical at times. Both invoke feelings in you that you might not necessarily know how to cope with. The fact of the matter is, there's quite a lot of overlap between thoughts and emotions. They're intertwined — often grotesquely fused together — and it's your job to pull them apart.

This is, of course, easier said than done. Your thoughts create your emotions, and your emotions create your thoughts. The problem is, your emotions can sometimes keep you from thinking rationally. If you're prone to overthinking, you're probably well aware of this! For a lot of us who overthink things, our thoughts are purely fear-based — meaning we cannot shake our thoughts free of fear. This typically ends up creating a stress response in your mind and body, and greatly contributes to the cycle of overthinking. Thankfully, though, breaking this cycle is totally possible. It's just a matter of being more mindful and learning how to regulate your emotions.

It can be challenging to wrap your head around the way your thoughts and emotions work, so I'll compare your thoughts to a forest fire that's fueled by your emotions — just to make things a bit more tangible. A thought could be like a spot of sunlight, shining through the treetops onto the dry brush at a very particular angle. This wouldn't necessarily start a fire right away, but let's say the dry brush is being blown about by the wind and air is exceptionally hot that day.

Let's say you've been going through a rough patch in a relationship. Once you've cooled down after having an argument, you might have a thought like: "I shouldn't have said that to my partner." This is sure to bring out some emotions — sadness, regret, anger, self-pity — which will undoubtedly spark more thoughts. "They're going to hate me, now. They're going to break up with me." These thoughts are going to spark more negative emotions, and so on and so forth.

Do you see how this cycle is like a forest fire? If you can't get your thoughts and emotions under control, they're going to keep spreading. They're going to destroy everything in their wake — *unless* you equip yourself with the tools needed to effectively fight them. What I'm trying to say is, all of us have the power to be metaphorical fire fighters. Mindfulness is a fire extinguisher, and self-care is the baking soda you sprinkle on top of the ashes.

Try to keep in mind that fighting your thoughts should be a **relaxed process**. You're not "fighting" them the same way you would fight an illness or a war. You're simply letting them wash over you. You're letting your thoughts and feelings happen, but you're not letting them control you. This takes practice, of course, but it can be immensely helpful in terms of relieving your stress.

*Reflection question: Where do my feelings come from?*

Gaining an understanding of where your feelings are coming from in the first place is a crucial step in eventually overcoming the thoughts that tend to send you into that vicious cycle of overthinking. When you experience a troubling thought, you can ask yourself: "okay, so where is this thought coming from?" Once you figure that out, you can say: "this is why I'm having this thought, but I don't have to let it build and grow."

People with overthinking tendencies often have the mindset that they *can't* control their thoughts. You might feel like you can't help overthinking about everything; that your thoughts just sort of happen and they're nothing you can do to stop them. I've been there too, so I get it! Your thoughts can make you feel like you're drowning. The thing is, you don't have to try to stop your thoughts from happening. They're going to happen no matter what. It's just a matter of learning how to swim against the current.

**Where Do Emotions Come From?**

Emotions can come from pretty much anywhere, but most of the time, they're born from a mixture of multiple different factors. Experts still have a lot to learn about how emotions work, as well as what we can do to properly regulate them. It's also worth mentioning that some people will have an easier time regulating their emotions than others. Emotional dysregulation is typically a trauma response. Those who suffer from disorders like PTSD and ADHD may especially struggle. Let's go over some of the main factors that may be triggering your emotional responses below:

### Physical State

Did you know that your physical state (i.e. the way your body feels) is heavily linked to your emotional state? When you're hungry or tired, for example, you might feel irritable or sad. At the same time, when you feel sad, your body might feel lethargic or achy. Your physical and emotional states are deeply intertwined, which is why it's so important to take care of your body as well as your mind.

You can even alter your emotional state by changing your posture. For example, if you slouch during a job interview, you're probably going to feel defeated. You might think to yourself: "I'm not going to get this job, so why even try in the first place?" If you sit up straight and make eye contact during your interview, however, you're probably going to feel a whole lot more confident — and this will show through to your potential employer.

Your physical state can also have an impact on the amount of neurotransmitters (like dopamine and serotonin) in your brain. If you've been to a doctor or therapist recently, they have recommended implementing a daily exercise regime into your routine. This is because physical exercise releases all of those feel-good neurotransmitters and hormones — dopamine, serotonin, endorphins, you name it — which in turn can reduce your stress and make you feel happier in general.

### Chemical Imbalances

The brain is awfully complicated, which means chemical imbalances are awfully common. Your various chemical imbalances could be contributing to your emotions more than you realize they are. Big emotions like sadness, anxiety, joy, and love are associated with specific neurotransmitters, so if these neurotransmitters are imbalanced, it can cause your emotions to go somewhat haywire.

If your serotonin levels are low, for example, you might feel more depressed or anxious than usual. Similarly, if you have a dopamine imbalance, you might not feel motivated to do the things you usually love doing. These feelings can often snowball into other feelings, which often sparks the overthinking cycle. You might think: "why am I feeling this way?" You might wonder why you can't bring yourself to paint, write, draw, or exercise. "These things are what make me happy, and I know that," you'll tell yourself as you lie awake at night. "So, why don't I want to do them?"

There are plenty of reasons why people experience chemical imbalances, the most common of which is genetics. Things like your diet, certain medications, and your environment can have a significant impact, too. Talking with a therapist and taking antidepressants or anti-anxiety medications can sometimes help those who suffer from chemical imbalances. Exercising every day can also help you regulate your emotions better, as can practicing mindfulness when your stressors get activated.

## Life Events

As human beings, a lot can happen to us throughout our lives. When you're a kid, you go through events like learning to ride a bike and losing your first tooth. Some kids may experience especially stressful events, like their parents getting divorced or their pets passing away. As you get older, you typically experience events like falling in love for the first time, getting your first job, and dealing with things like deaths in the family and financial difficulties.

Life events like this are *a lot* to cope with, especially for overthinkers. You might feel euphoric after your wedding and feel stressed out a week later because you realize you have to move and get a new job. You may also experience different strong emotions at different times about the same event. If you've ever gone through a rough breakup, for example, you might have felt relieved at first. Weeks after the breakup, however, you may have started missing your ex — despite the fact that the relationship was toxic. Brains are strange, and emotions often flip-flop! This is why it's so hard for overthinkers to regulate their emotions.

## What Are Emotions, Really?

Emotions can be scary and overwhelming, which is why it's common practice for people to avoid them. Understanding what emotions are and where they come from can help you learn to engage with them properly. This is not something most of us are taught growing up, the reason being that older adults (like your parents) oftentimes have trouble addressing and regulating their emotions as well.

Emotions are complicated, and it can be difficult to pinpoint which emotion or emotions you're feeling at any given time. Research suggests that there are ten primary emotions, namely fear, happiness, disgust, sadness, trust, distrust, shame, contempt, satisfaction, and amusement. There are then the emotions that branch off of these emotions (i.e. anger branches off of distrust and grief branches off of sadness). You can keep your emotions somewhat organized by thinking of them as an "emotional tree" of sorts.

Most of us have been taught to embrace our positive emotions and avoid our negative emotions, but this tendency to avoid can actually end up leading to an influx of emotional problems. You've probably heard that you shouldn't bottle up your bad feelings, as this only allows them to build up. This is basically the same principle. It's okay to feel that anger, shame, and fear — but don't let these emotions control you.

Come to think of it, you shouldn't let your positive emotions influence you too much either. Negative emotions can also masquerade as positive emotions, which is definitely something to be aware of. Let's say, for example, you quit your job because you were unhappy in that particular position. You might feel a boost of happiness and energy and go out drinking with your buddies to celebrate.

You might realize part way through the night, however, that you don't know what you're going to do now. You might start to feel some sadness and regret over quitting your job, especially if you needed that job to be able to pay your bills. Alcohol use can also force you to feel your negative emotions, but not in a particularly healthy way. Drinking because your sad is only going to make you feel more sad, so even if it works as a temporarily stress-reliever, I wouldn't recommend it.

Emotions, as you'll come to learn, are the messengers that inform you about your mental state. It's like when you scrape your knee and your pain receptors send a message to your brain that says: "*hey, you scraped your knee and it hurts!*" When you go through emotional pain, or "brain pain," your receptors react in a similar way. This happens because your brain is trying to protect you. It's saying: "*hey, the way you're feeling right now is emotionally painful!*"

Again, it's *a lot* to cope with. It really is. If your physical and emotional states are unbalanced, it can make things even more complicated. Your emotions can cause you to have misleading thoughts, which can lead you back to the cycle of overthinking you've become so familiar with. What can be done about this? Well, I'll get into that next.

*Reflection question: is it possible to feel consistently different (better) than how I do now?*

Learning how to properly regulate your emotions may seem insurmountable, and granted, it's hard work. Just the sheer thought of it makes a lot of people — especially overthinkers — freeze in their tracks. You're essentially training yourself to become a mindful thinker rather than an overthinker. Keep in mind that this takes practice, so if you do find yourself falling back into your overthinking habits even while trying to be mindful, don't be too hard on yourself about it. That's a part of being mindful, too!

So, how exactly should you go about regulating your emotions better? There's no cookie-cutter answer, and every person is different, but studies have shown that it can help to curate your thoughts. This involves learning how to properly focus your attention on the tidbits of actual useful information buried within your thoughts. It's sort of like digging for treasure. Every now and then, you'll strike gold! You just have to be mindful of the fact that sometimes you'll strike fools gold instead.

Learning how to curate your thoughts is all about being mindful of the things you think about, and how you think about them. Once you start to successfully curate your thoughts, you should find that you're able to think a lot more clearly as well as express yourself to others in a more effective way. This can be especially helpful for those with overthinking tendencies, as we tend to have a hard time expressing ourselves (what with all the thoughts bouncing around in our heads).

To curate your thoughts essentially means to think with intention. It means examining your mental and emotional state, and picking and choosing what you're going to focus on at any given moment. Scanning your mind and body is a big part of mindful meditation as well. It can help you feel grounded and in control, which should in turn help you gain control of your thoughts.

If you're going to get better at regulating your emotions, you're also going to want to start practicing self-care. You'd be surprised how much difference taking care of your body can make when it comes to your mental health. Staying hydrated, eating a proper diet, getting enough sleep, and exercising daily will — without question — make you feel better. Self-care takes work, though, and it can be difficult to establish a routine for yourself at first.

A lot of people who have trouble organizing their thoughts tend to have trouble staying organized in general. It makes sense. If you're unable to keep things straight in your head, it's not going to be very easy to keep things from going topsy-turvy in most areas of your life. Some find it helpful to keep a bullet journal, which can be an especially enjoyable way to organize your thoughts. Some come up with a meal plan and carry a water bottle around with them so that they don't fall behind on hydrating.

Finding a self-care routine that works for you can take some time, and the process is often one of trial and error. Keep in mind that it can take time for your body to adjust to a new routine. Mindful meditation, for example, can feel a bit silly at first — but you've got to stick with it. It won't do you any good to meditate for two minutes and then decide that it doesn't work for you. You haven't even given yourself a chance!

## Emotional Needs

Everyone has emotional needs. A common reason people may feel frustrated or dissatisfied with their lives is because these emotional needs aren't being met in one way or another. You've probably noticed how good it feels to be appreciated, to accomplish something, or to be accepted as part of a community. These things are quite emotionally nourishing to us! We drink them in like water, and thrive.

If you're feeling badly about something — or over-thinking about a certain situation — chances are, your emotional needs aren't being met. Everyone deserves to be loved and cherished; to feel safe, and to go through life with a sense of achievement and meaning. If you don't feel safe or secure in your life for any reason, this is a big problem that needs to be addressed right away. Not only is it keeping you from being happy, but your safety is on the line. Even if you're safe physically, feeling emotionally unsafe or insecure is ultimately going to keep you from living your life to the fullest.

Just remember to be kind to yourself. Take an hour or two out of each day for self-care, and put effort into connecting with the people you love. You might even find that by helping someone else meet their emotional needs, you can quench your own emotional needs. It's a win for everyone involved!

## Processing Unwanted Emotions

Experiencing unwanted emotions is just a part of being human, but that doesn't make the fact that you're experiencing them any less unpleasant. Learning how to properly process your emotions can be a challenge, but by utilizing the following strategies, you might just find that it's not as hard as you thought it would be. Check it out!

### *Identify Your Emotions*

If you're going to learn how to regulate your emotions, the first thing you'll want to do is identify them. Think to yourself: "what am I feeling right now," and label that feeling with an emotion. When you realize and name the fact that you're experiencing sadness, anxiety, anger, or distrust, it can make these emotions less intense.

### *Write it Down*

It may also be a good idea to write down your emotions and thoughts. Keeping a journal isn't for everyone, but if you have a tendency to overthink things, it's definitely worth a shot. Writing and making art in general is an excellent way to process your thoughts and emotions. You might discover a new passion for yourself!

### Talk to Someone

Have you ever talked to a friend or therapist about what you're going through and instantly felt like a weight was lifted off your chest? Even if you just need to vent about work, it's always helpful to have someone to talk to. Talking to a therapist in particular is a great way to process your thoughts and feelings, as therapists are literally professionally-trained to help you do so. You can also gain new perspectives from talking to others about your problems. Your friends and family members may have some surprisingly sound advice.

### Practice Mindfulness

Many people swear by doing a mindful meditation exercise, such as a body scan, every morning when you wake up. Being mindful is all about being present. When something is making you anxious, try to focus on your breathing and name what is happening in front of you right there and then. This is an excellent way to ground yourself when you can feel yourself entering the cycle of overthinking.

### Engage in Physical Activity

Whether it's running, swimming, or just going for daily walks, you can never go wrong with getting a little bit of exercise each day. It's a good idea to try to get into some sort of exercise routine. Try going for a jog when you wake up in the morning, or join a gym to keep yourself motivated! Exercising is hard at first, but it gets easier and the mental health benefits are absolutely worth it.

How you decide to process your thoughts and emotions is completely up to you. You may go through some trial and error as you find your footing, but you'll find something that works for you! Just be patient with yourself. As with anything else, these things take time and practice.

### Interactive Element

The only sure way to get better at regulating your emotions is to practice, practice, practice! Here are a few exercises you can do right now to sharpen up your emotion regulation skills:

### Make Room For Positive Experiences

Most people tend to focus on their negative experiences rather than their positive ones. This creates a general air of negativity, which can make you feel anxious and unhappy. Using the worksheet below, pick out at least one positive experience you can integrate into each day as a form of self-care. Use the blank spaces to come up with your own positive experiences:

| Going for a walk in the woods | Spending time creating something (drawing or writing, for example) | Read a book you've been meaning to read for a while | |
|---|---|---|---|
| Cooking your favorite meal | Do something nice for someone else | Watch your favorite t.v. show | |
| Spending time with a friend | Take a nice bubble bath | Meditate for half an hour | |

### Examining and Responding to Your Behaviors

When you feel sad, you typically become withdrawn or quiet. Similarly, when you feel angry, you might find yourself snapping at your friends or coworkers. Using the worksheet below, document your bad feelings and describe the behaviors that typically accompany them. Then, write about an opposite behavior, or a behavior that you'd like to act on instead (i.e. instead of snapping at your coworker, take a deep breath and go for a walk to cool down).

| | | |
|---|---|---|
| Angry/annoyed | | |
| Sad/upset | | |
| Scared/disgusted/fearful | | |

**Summary Box**

YOUR THOUGHTS and emotions are beautiful and complicated. Sometimes it feels like they're coming at you all at once! It's important to remember that you don't want to avoid your negative thoughts and emotions. In fact, it's best to acknowledge that they're happening, and that you're feeling a specific type of way. This will keep you grounded and help you feel more in control of your thoughts. The more you practice things like mindfulness and self-care, the easier this will get! Just stick with it.

## Segue

One of the main concerns people tend to have about breaking free from their overthinking habit is that they could possibly fall back into their old ways. Consider your life and the choices you've made thus far. You've got to be sure that you're overcoming your overthinking tendencies in a way that's actually effective — which is what we'll dive into next.

# 4

# THINK ENOUGH, BUT NOT TOO MUCH

*"In a moment of decision, the best thing you can do is the right thing to do, the next best thing is the wrong thing, and the worst thing you can do is nothing."*

— THEODORE ROOSEVELT

One of the biggest problems people with overthinking tendencies deal with is indecision. If your thoughts are disorganized, chances are your decision-making skills are going to take a hit. It doesn't help that you have to make a lot of important decisions when you're in your mid-twenties and early thirties, too! This is the age bracket where a lot of people go through things like career changes, health scares, and financial difficulties. It's also pretty common to get married and start having babies around this age, which is obviously a *huge* deal.

Interestingly, this age bracket also tends to be impacted by the most divorces. About 60% of divorces take place when both halves of the couple are between the ages of 25 and 39. One of the main reasons why this is the case probably has to do with the fact that life, when you're that age, can feel turbulent and unsteady. You're either in young adulthood, or you've just exited young adulthood. As much as you might *feel* like an adult (whatever that means), you've still got a lot to learn. You've still got to find your footing.

This, of course, involves making decisions that are likely going to have an impact on you for the rest of your life. This is understandably scary for a lot of young people. You might, for example, feel like you're deeply in love with the person you're dating at the age of 28, but when they propose, you start to feel a pit forming in the bottom of your stomach. You might ask yourself questions like: "do I really want to spend the rest of my life with this person?" and "what if it doesn't work out, and it was all just a big waste of time?"

It's perfectly valid to ask yourself questions like this. Getting married is a really big decision, and you want to be absolutely sure that it's the right decision for you and your partner. That said, decisions like this are a two-way street. Your partner might be all in on the idea of getting married or buying a house together, but you might not be so sure. And that's okay! The important thing is that you talk to your partner about it so that you can figure out a solution together.

Indecision and lack of communication skills oftentimes go hand-in-hand for people who overthink things. A friend of mine recently got into an argument with her husband because she was terrified by the idea of them buying a house together. It wasn't about the house, or her husband, necessarily. It was about the commitment. Not the mention the fact that houses are super expensive.

Instead of communicating her thoughts and feelings to her husband, though, she pretended like everything was fine and dandy, and that she was fully onboard with the plan. When the time came where she actually had to make a decision, however, she completely froze. Her husband wondered, at first, why she didn't seem to want the house anymore. All she had to tell him, though, was this: "I'm not ready."

Deciding that you're not ready to make that kind of decision yet is perfectly valid. In some cases, realizing that you're not ready to take that next step could be the best and most mature decision you end up making in your lifetime. It's a fine line to walk, though. That's what makes decision-making so complicated and nerve wracking. When making big decision, you need to be able to think logically and rationally. If you let too many "what ifs" cloud your judgment, you could potentially miss out on what could be a life-changing opportunity.

The question becomes: how do you know if you're making the right decision? The short answer is *you don't*, and that's okay! Life is all about taking leaps of faith, but if you overthink things too much, you'll just never know what life truly has in store for you. You'll get stuck in an endless state of analysis paralysis, always wondering "what if" but never taking any actual actions to achieve your goals.

*Reflection question: Where do I feel "stuck" in my life? (make a list)*

Have you ever felt paralyzed by the sheer idea of having to make a decision? You're definitely not alone. Every decision is like a great tree — branching off into hundreds of possibilities. This might be a little bit overwhelming, but just take a deep breath and keep reaching for the next branch. Don't look down and don't think too much about where the next foothold is going to be. Don't worry. You'll find a gnarled knot or a soft spot in the bark to support your weight while you climb.

Try to accept the fact that while climbing the decision tree, you might find yourself temporarily freezing up. This is normal, especially for those who have a fear of heights (in this case, overthinkers). Remember to be confident, and don't fret — for you are not truly stuck. It can sure as heck feel like you're stuck in the moment, though, so let's go over some strategies you can use to unfreeze yourself and keep moving forward when you get overwhelmed.

## How to Get Unstuck When You're Feeling Overwhelmed

There are a lot of things that can cause you to become "stuck," especially when it comes to making decisions that feel big and scary. Many overthinkers get stuck in a rut simply because they're too hard on themselves. Perhaps you've experienced this yourself. Let's say you've more than adequately prepared for an interview for a job you've always wanted, but while driving to the interview, your palms start to get sweaty. That voice in your head says: "Who are you kidding? You'll never get this job. You should turn around now and go home. Save yourself from the inevitable disappointment."

That voice is so mean, isn't it? Not to mention dramatic. When this voice begins to tickle at the back of your mind, it's perfectly okay to tell it to "shut up." It can't control you. It doesn't dictate what you can and can't do. It may seem like it's trying to protect you (i.e. "save yourself from the inevitable disappointment"), but this is not the case. Your inner critic, in a way, is responding to the fear and anxiety you might be feeling about the changes happening in your life. In other words, it's keeping you from living your life to the fullest.

Change is scary! I won't dispute that. All of us are constantly going through changes, big and small, all of the time. The world spins fast, and it can sometimes feel like too much is happening too soon — especially for those with overthinking tendencies. What a lot of people don't realize is, change doesn't just *happen*. It comes from within you. Changing is fundamentally what's going to get you out of your rut. It's just a matter of knowing how to change when you've been stuck for so long. Let's go over some strategies, shall we?

### Start Small

ONE OF THE reasons people find change scary is that most people thrive on routine. The idea of changing up a routine you've been following for years can be pretty intimidating, but here's the good news: you don't have to change everything all at once. Start by making small changes to your daily routine. For example, if you order takeout or delivery most days, choose one or two days out of the week where you cook your own meals instead. Making small changes like this will help give you the courage you need to start making big changes in your life.

### Change Your Perspective

Taking a break from your daily routine once in a while is a great way to eventually break out of it. Introducing things like meditation, regular exercise, and healthy eating into your routine can help you gain new perspectives (as well as make new friends)! Opening your mind to new experiences and different perspectives is one of the most important parts of changing. It can help you gain insight on what's actually possible for your future as well as give you the confidence you need to achieve your goals.

## Explore What Your Purpose Is

Feeling like your life has purpose is a crucial emotional need for most people. Take some time to consider what really makes you happy, and what has made you feel fulfilled in the past. Maybe you used to volunteer at an animal shelter, or perhaps you spent one night a week serving dinner at a soup kitchen when you were a teenager trying to beef up your college applications. Consider and reflect upon what made you lose sight of your true purpose in life, and do what you need to do to gain that sense of purpose back.

## Believe in Yourself

You've probably heard this one before, but that's just because it's really good advice! People who seem to have it all figured out will usually tell you that life is about 90% confidence. There's quite a bit of truth to this. Forcing yourself to step outside of your comfort zone once in a while can make you feel like you can truly do anything you set your mind to — and you absolutely can! Believing in yourself often requires retraining your brain. The first thing you'll want to do is stop saying things like: "I can't do this" or "I'm not good enough." The fact of the matter is, you really don't know what you can and cannot do until you try.

*Let Go of Your Past*

Whatever may have happened in the past cannot be undone. If you're constantly ruminating on mistakes you made years ago, you're going to have a hard time being happy in life. Some mistakes — and some trauma — can be especially hard to live with. I completely get it. However, forgiving yourself (and others), and letting go of the mistakes you made in your past is a necessary part of changing for the better and finding happiness. Consider this quote from the hit 2014 television show *Bojack Horseman*: "It takes a long time to realize how truly miserable you are and even longer to see that it doesn't have to be that way. Only after you give up everything can you begin to find a way to be happy."

## How Do You Know When You Have Enough Information to Make a Smart Decision?

In this day and age, most people get the majority of their information from the internet. This honestly isn't great, but the internet can actually be helpful if you know where to look. When gathering information to help you make an informed decision about something, it's a good idea to take a few different factors into consideration. You should start by analyzing the possible outcomes of the decision you're trying to make.

Some find it helpful to make a list of the various pros and cons!

You should also trust your gut when it comes to the quality of the information you're seeking. If your body is trying to tell you something is off about the information you've gathered, try to seek out other, more credible information from a better source. In general, you'll know whether or not you've gathered enough information to make a decision based on how confident you're feeling about it.

Try to keep in mind, however, that with every decision comes a leap of faith. Gathering information simply makes the gap you have to leap over a bit smaller.

## How to Make Good Decisions

Like most adult human beings, you've probably had to make hundreds of decisions throughout your life already. Some of these decisions have been small (i.e. having to decide what you want to eat for dinner), while others have undoubtedly been massive (i.e. "Should I marry this person?" "Should I quit my job?") Making decisions is hard, and you can't always know in the moment whether the decision you're making is a good one.

When making an important decision, you've got to remember not to let your stress influence you too much. It'll be there, for sure, but you don't have to let it send you into a state of analysis paralysis. Just take a deep breath. Everything will be okay. If possible, you should also give yourself some time and space to really think about the decision you're trying to make. Go for a walk, and weigh your options. Try to remain calm so that you can think rationally about this.

It might also be helpful to get another person's perspective on the decision you have to make. Gaining outside perspectives from your friends and family members can help you see your situation in a brand new light. Talking these things out can also help you process your thoughts and feelings, which means you'll be able to make your final decision with a clear head. Remember to trust your gut and take a leap of faith. No matter what you decide, it'll be well worth it in the end.

## How to Be Agile and Responsive When Life Gets Tough

People who overthink things tend to freeze up when life gets exceptionally difficult. This is part of the "fight, flight, or freeze" response system your body uses when you're faced with something that makes you fearful.

Learning how to be agile and responsive when dealing with something scary takes a lot of time and effort, but it's definitely worth it. One helpful thing you can do when faced with tough situations is a risk assessment. I'll go over how to do a risk assessment below to make things a bit easier.

## How to Do a Basic Risk Assessment or Analysis

### 1. Identify the Hazards

Each decision you make comes with its own set of potential hazards, and it's important to do your best to identify them. This is mostly a matter of trial and error and gathering necessary information. Before you serve peanut butter cookies to your friend, for example, you should double-check whether or not they have a peanut allergy.

### 2. Consider Who May Be Harmed and How

It's always a good idea to think about who your decision-making process will impact, both positively and negatively. Let's say, for example, that you're trying to decide whether or not to move out of your parents' house, get married and get an apartment with your partner. While this may hurt your parents' feelings, it's probably going to be the best option for your mental health, your romantic relationship, and your future as a functioning adult.

### 3. Evaluate and Remove the Risks if Possible

Let's build on the example from above: you're moving out of your parents' house, and this hurts them because it makes them feel as if you don't like living with them or that you don't need them anymore. You might worry that moving out will damage your relationship with your parents, but you shouldn't let this worry keep you from moving out. That will only cause resentment to build. Talk to your parents. Let them share their feelings, and then share your own perspective on the matter. You should eventually be able to find some common ground.

### 4. Record Your Thoughts

As always, it's a good idea to keep a record of your thoughts and feelings. Writing down what you're feeling about making a certain decision can help clear out any brain fog, meaning you'll be able to make your final decision with a clear mind. This should also help you stay organized. A journal is a great place to make a pros and cons list as well as write out any complicated emotions you might be having about the potential consequences of making your decision.

## Contingency Planning

Sometimes, things don't pan out the way you want them to. Perhaps you didn't end up acing that job interview, or maybe you went on a date that ended in disaster. Either way, when making plans and decisions, it's always smart to have some sort of back-up plan in place. Contingency planning can also help you remedy the anxiety that often comes with making decisions. When you have a plan b, you won't have to worry about what might happen if your original plan doesn't work out.

*Reflection question: Where is fear keeping you stuck or holding you back in your life?*

## Fear-setting

While doing my research, I learned about a method called "fear-setting." Employing fear-setting (a method created by Tim Ferriss) into your daily life can help you handle high-stress situations and eliminate analysis paralysis. To put it simply, fear-setting is visualizing all of the bad things that could possibly happen in any given situation, therefore making it possible for you to move forward with making difficult decisions without your fear and anxiety getting in the way.

Fear-setting has a lot to do with stoicism, which is essentially the concept of enduring pain without displaying the fact that said pain is bothering you. Practicing stoicism can basically trick your brain into thinking painful experiences actually *don't* bother you. Mind over matter, you know?

**Interactive Element**

I'd like to give you an opportunity to practice a little bit of fear-setting right now. Using the worksheet below, define the worst things that could possibly happen to you. In the next column, list the ways in which you could potentially stop these bad things from happening. In the last column, list how you will repair each bad thing if it does end up happening.

| Define | Prevent | Repair |
|--------|---------|--------|
|        |         |        |
|        |         |        |
|        |         |        |
|        |         |        |

**Summary Box**

MAKING DECISIONS IS NEVER EASY, especially for overthinkers. When it feels like your thoughts are all over the place, it can be difficult to make a decision that's based on logic and reason — meaning you may risk making a potentially wrong decision. Thankfully, though, there are plenty of strategies you can use to make decisions more effectively. It's also important to consider the fact that a lot of people who have difficulties making decisions are afraid of change. This fear of change is the reason overthinkers often find themselves stuck in a rut. However, it doesn't have to be this way! By changing up your routine, opening your mind to other perspectives, and employing methods like contingency planning and fear-setting, you can conquer your fears and become a better decision-maker.

**Segue**

Overthinking everything all the time is not just exhausting — it's also incredibly overwhelming. Being overwhelmed can occasionally cause you to act irrationally. You might find yourself snapping at your loved ones or breaking down in the middle of a workday. In the next section of this book, I'll talk about what you can do to reclaim your life when it feels like you're drowning in the overwhelm.

**Here's the thing: you can help others by leaving an honest review of this life-changing book. And the best part? It won't cost you a dime.**

So let me ask you this: would you help someone you've never met, if it didn't cost you money and you never got credit for it? If so, here's your chance. You can help someone just like you, who's seeking information but unsure where to look. You can be the one to guide them towards this incredible resource.

By leaving a review, you can help:

- One more person conquer their anxiety
- One more person get a good night's sleep
- One more person make confident decisions
- One more person live a life free of negative thoughts

And all it takes is less than 60 seconds of your time.

If you're listening to the audiobook, simply hit the three dots in the top right of your device, click rate & review, then leave a few sentences about the book with a 5-star rating. If you're reading on Kindle or an e-reader, scroll to the bottom of the book, then swipe up and it will automatically prompt a review. And if for some reason the functionality has changed, you can go to the book page on Amazon or wherever you purchased the book and leave a 5-star review there.

By helping others, you're also helping yourself. People who help others (with zero expectation) experience higher levels of fulfillment, live longer, and make more money. So why not make a difference in someone else's life today?

Thank you from the bottom of my heart. Now, back to conquering overthinking!

## 5

## END THE OVERWHELM

*"Nothing can harm you as much as your own thoughts unguarded."*

— BUDDHA

For those of us with overthinking tendencies, it's quite easy to want to curl up into a little ball and not talk to anyone for hours on end. Like anyone else, we have our especially bad days. Oftentimes, our thoughts are so intense and plentiful that they tire us out. If you've ever felt overwhelmed and exhausted by your thoughts, just know you're not alone in feeling like this.

By now, you're probably well aware of how emotionally labor-intensive the cycle of overthinking can actually be. Not only is it overwhelming, but it can also be quite isolating. It can make you feel like you're "losing it" in the most invisible sort of way. You're slipping through the cracks, and at times it feels like no one cares or even notices how much pain you're in.

It's quite normal to feel helpless when you get trapped in the cycle of overthinking, but I want you to know that snapping out of it (so to speak) is totally possible. Keep in mind that *you're* the boss of your own thoughts. *You're* the one who's in control here. Are you ready to reclaim your life?

*Reflection question: How often do I feel life is too much for me?*

You know when you're lying in bed at night, staring at the ceiling and listening to your thoughts get louder and louder in your mind? So much for sleeping. Your brain is wide awake, and it thinks you should be too. Never mind the fact that it's two in the morning and your partner fell asleep the second their head hit their pillow.

All you want to do is sleep, but your thoughts are practically bouncing off the walls. You're deep into the overthinking cycle, needlessly stressing about tomorrow and the next day and the day after that. It almost feels like your brain *has* to have something to stress about, or else it can't function properly. "This is just how I operate," you'll tell yourself and others, half-joking, half-serious. "I'm a perfectionist."

Being a "perfectionist" is all good and well — and hey, it's a great look for job interviews — but (as a perfectionist myself), I've noticed that people with this particular personality trait often overdo it by quite a lot. Perfectionists also tend to be really, really hard on themselves. Let's say, for example, that you work in an office building. You show up to work fifteen minutes early every day with not a single hair out of place. You do your work without error, socialize cordially with your coworkers at lunchtime, and go above and beyond without making a big deal about it.

Any yet... nobody seems to appreciate all that you do. You think to yourself "this company would fall apart without me." When you get home from work, you pour yourself a glass of wine. Your eye starts to twitch. "Imagine if I just didn't show up for work tomorrow?" The thought makes you giddy, but you'll never actually do such a thing. Even if your job makes you miserable, you'll show up in the morning, fifteen minutes early like you always do.

I'm not trying to call anyone out, by the way. It's just that there's something very wrong with this picture, but it can be difficult to see that when you're the one living this kind of life. A friend of mine once told an interviewer that she "thrives in chaos" and she got the job. I found this funny because although "thriving in chaos" is a heavily wanted trait in workers (especially in fast-paced work environments), nobody actually thrives in chaos.

My friend was a high-functioning overwhelmed overthinker, which means she worked herself half to death before realizing she was harming herself more than helping herself. We're humans, not robots! If you robotize yourself, people are going to think they can take advantage of you. If you use your overwhelmed feelings to fuel your own robotization, you're never going to have the time to take a rest and actually address those feelings.

Mental overwhelm, as it turns out, is a bit complicated. Most of us know what it's like to be overwhelmed, but very few of us know how to calm down when we get overwhelmed. Stick around, because that's what we're going to examine next!

## What is Mental Overwhelm?

When a circuit breaker gets overloaded with electricity, it tends to immediately shut down. The system essentially gets overwhelmed because it's trying to handle way too much. Your brain and body works in a very similar way. If you have too much on your plate, or there are too many thoughts bouncing around in your head, you're going to have a difficult time functioning.

Mental overwhelm is an emotional state that you're probably quite familiar with if you're prone to overthinking. When something feels too challenging — when life starts to feel like all too much — your brain and body go into panic mode. You might feel like your heart is beating too fast or like you're on the verge of tears all of a sudden. You might snap at your coworkers or your significant other, or break down when someone asks you if you're okay.

Being overwhelmed is more than just being stressed out. When you're overwhelmed, you feel like you're being buried alive by your thoughts — which is a terrifying experience. Because your thoughts are so all over the place, you might find that you have a hard time verbalizing *why*, exactly, you're feeling this way. When someone asks you "what's wrong," you might burst into tears and say: "I don't know!"

Coping with being overwhelmed can be challenging, but it's definitely possible if you have the right tools on hand. Realizing that you're overwhelmed and naming that feeling is a good place to start. When you begin to feel stress building up in your brain and body, take a deep breath and repeat this mantra in your head: *I'm just feeling overwhelmed right now, but it's only temporary. This too shall pass.* If you can, remove yourself from any high-stress situations or environments you might be in. If there's a problem you need to solve, you can enter back into that space when you're ready.

## Why Too Much Complexity Leads to Mental Breakdown

The world (and adult life in general) is far more complicated than it used to be. As millennials, we've been through a lot in our short lives — extreme political divide, people's rights getting taken away, a global pandemic, climate change, extreme inflation in conjunction with working wages that frankly aren't livable in this economy — you name it. Our current society is ruled by social media and automation. It's a drastic change, and this change is taking place during our most formative years. Of *course* we're overwhelmed.

Feeling like the world is in shambles tends to ignite a heavy sense of despair, which most people aren't equipped to deal with. This despair oftentimes turns to anger, and anger eventually dissipates into defeat. And so, you become complacent. You go through the motions, waltzing through this topsy-turvy world on autopilot. When you're in a constant state of overwhelm, it's difficult to know what else you're supposed to do.

I'm here to tell you that you don't have to live like

this. There may be a number of reasons life feels too complicated for you to properly handle, but there's one reason in particular that a lot of people don't take into consideration: you're actually adding to your own overwhelm. Now, this is not your fault. The world *is* complicated, so it's only natural for your life to be complicated as well — especially considering the fact that society is built on capitalism and productivity is valued over everything else.

It might be difficult to pinpoint how exactly you're making your life more complicated than it needs to be, so let's break it down below:

## 1. You're Constantly Worrying

Worrying drains your energy, so if you're constantly worrying, chances are you're going to feel exhausted most of the time. A lot of people with overthinking tendencies spend more time worrying about the future than they do living in the moment. Let's say, for example, you're attending your mom's sixtieth birthday party and everyone around you seems to be happy and stress-free. Meanwhile, instead of celebrating with everyone else, you're worrying about the presentation you have to give at work next week. So, you see? Worrying too much is preventing you from actually living your life.

## 2. You're Trying to Control Everything in Life

Everyone wants to feel like they have some semblance of control in their lives. Many people end up burying their fears in order to avoid facing them, which can provide a temporary illusion of control. However, the truth is, if you feel like you need to control absolutely everything in your life, you're letting your fear control you. The need for control comes from a place of fear, after all. There's a reason our previous president behaved the way he did while in office. Once you learn to accept that you can't control everything, you'll be significantly happier.

## 3. You're Basing Your Happiness on the Happiness of Others

If you want to find happiness, that happiness has got to come from you. You've undoubtedly seen your friends posting on social media about how gosh dang wonderful their lives are, and perhaps this has made you feel insecure. You might think: "how does this person already have a house and a husband and a baby? I can barely pay rent for my apartment!" What you've got to realize is that the happiness and success of others has nothing to do with your own happiness and success. Comparing yourself to others is only going to make you more dissatisfied. Take a breath, and maybe take a break from social media for a while. This is your life, and you get to decide how you want to live it.

## What Are the Signs That a Breakdown is Imminent?

What is a nervous breakdown? Why do nervous breakdowns happen? The term "nervous breakdown" actually has a bit of a negative connotation these days, but it's still widely used by the public to describe what happens when a person loses their ability to function due to a mental health crisis. When you're having a mental health crisis, you might feel like you have a total lack of control. You may find it difficult to function at work as well as do things like eat, sleep, and communicate with others.

Having a mental health crisis is a scary experience, but if you're aware of the signs, you might just be able to stop it from happening. When you're on the edge of a mental health crisis, you'll probably start feeling some symptoms of anxiety — such as nausea, trouble breathing, and cold sweats. You might feel dizzy or like your heart is beating inside of your throat. If you can, sit down and ask someone for a glass of water. Tell yourself: "this too shall pass," and try to focus on your breathing.

Those who are at risk of having a breakdown typically start showing signs days in advance. They might miss social events they had previously claimed they were looking forward to, or they might call out from work multiple days in a row. People in the midst of a mental health crisis tend to isolate themselves and skip out on things like exercising and practicing proper hygiene. Why, you might ask? Because when you're having a breakdown, doing these things feels impossible.

There are a number of things that can cause someone to experience a mental health crisis. When you go through something traumatic, such as a bad breakup or the loss of a loved one, your various systems tend to get overloaded and eventually shut down. Breakdowns like this are unpleasant, but they're treatable. A combination of cognitive behavioral therapy and medication has been proven to be quite beneficial for most.

*Reflection question: Can I recognize when I am overwhelmed and create a plan of action to quickly depressurize when it occurs?*

Consider what happens when a pressure cooker has too much pressure building up inside of it. Eventually, the stress becomes too much for it to handle and it blows its lid. In order to keep your beans or delicious stew from splattering all over your kitchen, you need to make sure that your pressure cooker is actually able to release pressure.

The question is, when you're overloaded with stress, how should you go about depressurizing yourself? Let's say you have a high-pressure job where people are demanding things of you all day every day. After a certain point, you might feel like you're going to explode. Any person would. Like I mentioned before, we're humans, not robots. When you feel this way, it can be helpful to have some strategies on hand to create immediate ease. This can be achieved by simplifying your life and giving yourself some room to breathe.

If you feel like you have too much on your plate, take a beat and consider this: what can I drop, defer, or delegate? If you have an onslaught of unproductive meetings on your schedule, for example, you should go ahead and drop those. They're time-wasters, anyway, and are only contributing to your stress. Consider which tasks need to be done right now, and which tasks are less urgent. Defer your less urgent tasks until a later date, and focus on what needs to be done in the moment. This will help you stay organized, focused, and calm. You can also delegate important tasks, which essentially means entrusting others around you to complete the tasks you simply don't have time for. Remember: there's nothing wrong with asking for help when you need it!

## How to Simplify Your Life

Like most human beings, your life is probably chock-full of things to do, places to go, and people to see. It's normal to feel overwhelmed by all of this, especially when more things keep getting added to your already full plate. Contrary to popular belief, it is actually okay to not finish everything that's been placed in front of you. It's really not the end of the world, and everything will be okay. Ask a friend or a coworker to help you eat if it feels like too much to consume on your own. After all, overeating can make you sick.

Simplifying your life is all about removing distractions and unnecessary tasks. It's a big part of taking care of your mental health and practicing self-care. Try to think of your life as a cluttered work desk. If your desk becomes too cluttered, how are you supposed to get any work done? If you're not sure where to start, try making a list of all of the things in your life that feel like clutter. For example, if you have an in-person meeting scheduled with a client that could easily be covered by sending a simple email, cancel the meeting and send the email. Your client will probably appreciate it as well!

One of the most common reasons people feel stressed out is because they're trying to chase too many goals at once. Consider your list of goals, and simplify it. Removing certain goals from your list doesn't mean you'll never achieve them, it just means you don't have to achieve them *right now*. Using fewer words and not engaging with drama can also be quite beneficial when you're trying to simplify your life. You might be tempted to talk with your coworkers about who got the receptionist pregnant, but that's clutter. It's *junk food*. You'll be much happier if you mind your own business. Just do you!

You can also effectively manage your stress by dividing up your various tasks into more manageable chunks. This can be especially helpful for people with mental health issues like generalized anxiety and ADHD. Consider Cinderella: her evil step-mother gives her a long list of things to do every day. She shouldn't have to do all of these ridiculous tasks, but she kind of has to — at least until her prince comes around and has her try on the glass slipper.

I've always found it kind of amazing that Cinderella is able to look at this long list of tasks and just do them, but perhaps she's able to get everything done because she does one task at a time and breaks her work into more manageable parts. When you've got a lot on your plate, don't look at all of the food at once. This will only create more stress. Work on the side dish first, then the salad, *then* the main course. You'll thank yourself for taking it slow, and you should have no problem cleaning your plate in the end.

**Summary Box**

BEING OVERWHELMED IS AN UNPLEASANT FEELING, but it's important to keep in mind that it's not a feeling that will last forever. By decluttering and simplifying your life, you can avoid entering the realm of overwhelm, meaning you'll be that much closer to achieving peace and happiness. Remember: you don't have to control everything in your life, and the way others are seemingly living their lives has nothing to do with you. When you feel like you're in danger of having a mental health crisis, sit down, drink some water, and take a deep breath. Remember: *This too shall pass!*

**Segue**

When anxiety kicks in, what should you do? Effectively coping with anxiety takes time and practice, but with the right tools and strategies, you should find that your anxiety is more manageable than you thought it was. In the next section, I'll discuss some strategies you can use to calm down quickly in the event of an upcoming anxiety attack. These strategies have worked well for Lauren and I, and I hope you'll find them helpful as well!

# 6

# FAST CALM

*"Worrying does not take away tomorrow's troubles; it takes away today's peace."*

— RANDY ARMSTRONG

There's not exactly an end-all, be-all "cure" for overthinking, but there *is* a pretty decent "first aid kit" of sorts you can carry around with you. This first aid kit should help keep you calm when you enter the overthinking cycle and begin to feel overwhelmed. Try to keep in mind that first aid kits come with "fast fixes" for injuries — such as bandages, gauze, cleansing wipes, and antiseptic cream. These things can be incredibly helpful, but if your injury is serious, you should really go to the doctor after dressing your wound.

It's the same with mental health. When your sympathetic nervous system gets triggered by a stressful event, the best thing you can do to calm down is engage your parasympathetic system. I'll discuss how you can do this in a minute, but I just want to stress the importance of seeking help from a mental health professional if you want to do more than just put a bandaid over your emotional cut.

Before we get into the ins and outs of the sympathetic nervous system and the parasympathetic nervous system, let's do a deep dive into something called the "fight-or-flight" response. The fight-or-flight response is a fascinating psychological phenomenon that tends to occur when you're faced with a stressful event or situation.

When I was eight or nine years old, one of the kids in my neighborhood used to ride barefoot on the spokes of my bike. This was obviously a bad idea, but we were just kids. We didn't really take the time to think about what could possibly go wrong. Anyway, one day, I took a spill while my friend was — you guessed it — standing barefoot on my bicycle spokes. His foot got torn open, so much so that the bone was sticking out.

I remember screaming and running to go get my mom. Even at that young age, this wild event triggered my fight-or-flight response. In retrospect, I probably shouldn't have left my friend lying there with his bone out, but I had to get help. It also made me pretty sick to my stomach, seeing his bone sticking out like that. I couldn't help it. It was just how my body responded.

Thankfully, my friend was okay. His parents got him to the hospital as quickly as they could, and he eventually recovered. It just goes to show that it's amazing what the human body is capable of, especially when it comes to healing itself. The same can be said about the human brain. No matter what you've been through — no matter how you responded to certain events in the past — healing is always possible.

There are three basic stages of the fight-or-flight response you should be aware of, namely the alarm stage, the resistance stage, and the exhaustion stage. If you've ever had to bring a friend or loved one to the E.R., or have found yourself in an emergency situation, you're probably well aware of these stages. Just for kicks (and to make things a little easier to understand), let's explore these stages by looking at a potential scenario.

Let's say you're going on a hike with your friends in the woods when all of a sudden you come upon a mountain lion. You're in the middle of nowhere — miles away from your car in the parking lot — and the hungry lioness seems to be stalking you. Each person in your friend group is going to experience either a fight-

or-flight response to this event. Some will turn and run, which, just to be clear, is *not* what you should do if you come face-to-face with a mountain lion. Some might try to make themselves large, or throw rocks at the mountain lion to try to get it to go away. These actions illustrate what generally happens during the alarm and resistance stages of a person's fight-or-flight response.

After everything is said and done, you'll enter the exhaustion stage. It's pretty common for people to cry during this stage, as it typically ignites a sense of grief mixed with relief. Perhaps the mountain lion left you and your friends alone, but not before it bit someone on the ankle. You've got to rush that person to the emergency room now, but hey, at least everyone survived.

## The Sympathetic Nervous System and the Parasympathetic Nervous System

The fight-or-flight response, as you may have guessed, has to do with the body's sympathetic nervous system. During sudden and stressful events, your body releases hormones that trigger the sympathetic nervous system to have a particular response. The hormones that get released are meant to prepare you to either fight your way out of the situation or run away to protect yourself from harm.

Your body can stay in a state of fight-or-flight for 20 to 60 minutes after the threat has already dissipated. This can be pretty unpleasant, but don't worry. Your parasympathetic nervous system will eventually return to its normal hormonal levels, which means you'll finally be able to calm down. This is why it's recommended to activate your parasympathetic system whenever you find yourself in a situation that's stressing you out.

The thing is, it's pretty rare to find yourself in a situation where it's actually necessary to fight or flee. When your body senses that you're scared or stressed out for any reason, however, it'll begin to enter into that fight-or-flight state. To put it simply, your body often overreacts to stressors that aren't actually that big of a deal. This is where activating your parasympathetic nervous system can really come in handy.

## How Activating Your Parasympathetic Nervous System Can Lower Stress

While the sympathetic nervous system prepares you to deal with stressful events, the parasympathetic system is what helps you de-stress. The question is: how do you go about activating your parasympathetic nervous system? It's not like there's some sort of on-and-off switch for these kinds of things, however, engaging your parasympathetic nervous system is more simple than most people realize.

Needless to say, the world we're living in is a stressful one. Because of this, your fight-or-flight response is essentially on standby. For young women in particular, just walking down the street by yourself at night can be a scary experience. Women have been taught that they need to be in a constant state of alert — and for a good but unfortunate reason. The women in my life, Lauren included, have told me about how they have to hold their keys between their fingers when they walk anywhere alone, which is obviously astonishing. Nobody should have to live in fear like that. Nobody should have to feel like they're constantly in danger.

Being in a constant state of alert can cause one's sympathetic nervous system to go somewhat haywire. Your blood pressure rises, and your heart rate goes up. Your pupils dilate, and your palms begin to sweat. Everyone and everything around you could be a potential threat, and so you must always be prepared to go into fight-or-flight mode. At least, that's what your brain and body is telling you. This is especially true if you're prone to overthinking.

That said, it's not like the dangers aren't there. We've all heard stories about young women getting abducted, assaulted, or worse. This is disproportionately true for women of color, who have to deal with an intricate and especially dangerous subset of misogyny. The fact of the matter is, carrying pepper spray is always a good idea when you're in an unfamiliar environment. This is true regardless of gender, but until men learn to act like civilized human beings, women will always have to be that much more aware of their surroundings.

That said, as a young woman, when you get to where you're going, you should be able to let your guard down a little bit — especially if you're meeting up with your friends or your significant other. Even when you get to a safe environment, however, your fight-or-flight response may continue to act up. This is when it's a good idea to engage your parasympathetic nervous system in order to get yourself to calm down a little bit.

*Reflection question: How can I be more mindful of when I am being triggered into fight-or-flight?*

## How to Engage Your Parasympathetic Nervous System

Your parasympathetic nervous system is responsible for the "rest and digest" response that takes place in your body after you've endured a particularly stressful event. By participating in activities that lower your heart rate and decrease your blood pressure, you can activate your parasympathetic nervous system all on your own. The next time you're feeling stressed out, try out one of these quick strategies to help yourself calm down. You should start feeling better straight away!

### Stick Your Face in Cold Water

This may sound a bit odd, but putting your face into a basin of cold water when you're feeling stressed out can actually trigger a physiological response. This method has actually been scientifically proven to stimulate the parasympathetic nervous system. In short, it distracts your brain and body from the fact you're stressed out, meaning your parasympathetic system will be like "oh, okay, time to calm down now." This is why people often splash cold water on their face when they're stressing about something!

### Stay Hydrated

DRINKING plenty of water throughout the day is one of the best things you can do for your mind and body. The next time you're feeling anxious, pour yourself a nice glass of ice water and drink it slowly. I recommend sitting outside while you drink, especially if the weather's nice. You can never go wrong with fresh water and fresh air, don't you think?

### Spend Time Outside

There's a reason people say things like "I need to take a walk" when they're feeling stressed out. Spending time outside, breathing in the fresh air and communing with nature is a great way to calm yourself down. Not only does being outside activate your parasympathetic nervous system, but it can also help you notice all of the beauty in the world. It can make help you gain a bit of perspective and make you feel like maybe it's not the end of the world after all.

### Distract Your Mind

When my wife gets trapped in the overthinking cycle, she often asks me to tell her some jokes. I can't tell you how many times I've frantically googled "jokes" on my phone. I also can't even begin to describe how helpful this has been in a pinch! Things like watching movies, listening to music, and singing can also be great distractions when you're feeling stressed out.

### Chant a Mantra

Saying a mantra or two out loud (or in your head) can work wonders. The next time you start to get anxious, try saying one of these mantras:

- "My body deserves time to rest and recharge."
- "When I take deep, conscious breaths, my body relaxes."
- "I won't pressure myself, I'll simply listen to my own body."

Saying and repeating mantras while focusing on your breathing is a form of mindful meditation. By convincing your brain that you are, in fact, calm, you can easily calm yourself down. Keep in mind that you may have to repeat your favorite mantra over and over again. Most of the time it won't start working right away, but within a few minutes, you should start to feel better.

## *Laugh*

DID you know that laughing is super good for your health? This is why getting someone to tell you jokes or watch a funny video can be so helpful when you're feeling stressed out. Laughter has been proven to engage your parasympathetic nervous system, so the next time you're feeling a little bit on edge, try putting on an episode of your favorite comedy show and laugh it up!

## *Move or Jump Around*

Engaging in physical exercise releases your excess adrenaline and increases endorphins (happy hormones) in your body. When you're feeling especially anxious, you might be able to destress by running around the block or doing some jumping jacks. This will get your blood pumping, as well as help you calm down a bit.

## *Get Some Perspective*

I always find it helpful to put things into perspective. When you're feeling anxious about something, your problems can seem huge. Many overthinkers develop a sort of tunnel vision for their problems. They become all that's visible. They become all that matters in that particular moment! However, if you take a step back and put things into perspective, your problems won't feel so big anymore. Remember: you've overcome worse situations before, and you'll overcome this as well.

### Practice Belly Breathing

Belly breathing engages your diaphragm, and is an excellent method to use if you feel like you're having trouble breathing as a result of an anxiety attack. When you breathe normally, your breaths are actually quite shallow — and anxiety can make this even worse. I recommend practicing belly breathing for about 5 to 10 minutes every day. Here's how to do it:

- Lie down on your bed with a pillow underneath both your head and your knees. It's important that you find a comfortable position.
- Place one of your hands on your upper chest, right in the middle. Place your other hand on your stomach, just below your rib cage and right above your diaphragm.

- Slowly breathe in through your nose, drawing in breath towards your stomach. You should feel your stomach pushing upward against your hand while inhaling.
- When you exhale, your abdominal muscles should tighten and your stomach should fall downwards. Let the air out through pursed lips and repeat this process as many times as you need to.

### Acu/Pressure

Applying pressure to certain points on your body can help significantly when it comes to reducing stress and anxiety. Here's one easy pressure point exercise you can try right now:

- Sit in a comfortable position. Use pillows to support your neck and back if you need to. It can also be helpful to close your eyes while you do this exercise.
- Gently touch the spot between your eyebrows with your thumb or index finger.
- While taking slow, deep breaths, apply gentle pressure to that spot in a circular motion for 5 to 10 minutes.

### Allow Yourself to Cry

Laughing and crying are actually quite similar, so it's no surprise that crying is good for you as well. Crying can be an alleviating, purifying experience for most people. It releases tension and makes you feel better when you're in a state of overwhelm. Some people might tell you that crying is weak, but that couldn't be further from the truth! Crying is perfectly human. You should always cry if that's what you need to do.

### Create or Do

Engaging in something you're passionate about is an excellent stress-management technique. Not only does it distract your mind, but it also makes you happy. Creating art or writing is also a great way to process your emotions. If you're not particularly experienced when it comes to creating, don't worry. Just give it your best shot! You might even discover a new passion for yourself.

### Interactive Element

Here are a couple of quick fixes for you to try out when you're feeling stressed or anxious. Keep in mind that these exercises are just suggestions, and you can tweak them however you see fit.

1. Go outside and write down everything you see that's the color orange. Use this worksheet if you'd like!

_____

2. Use the box below to draw how you're feeling. Don't be afraid to get creative with it!

**Summary Box**

THE REASON you get anxious and overwhelmed largely has to do with the hormones your body releases during stressful events. Your sympathetic nervous system prepares your body to go into a fight-or-flight response — meaning you'll either fight or flee when you find yourself in a situation that your mind and body perceive as dangerous. Your parasympathetic nervous system is what calms you down when the threat in question dissipates. There are a number of methods you can use to activate your parasympathetic nervous system when you're feeling anxious. Some of the best ways to do so include going outside, taking belly breaths, and submerging your face in cold water.

## Segue

Why do you often find yourself getting trapped in an overthinking loop? What triggers your state of over-thinking in the first place? These are both excellent questions, and it's what we're going to dive into next, so stick around!

# 7

# TRIGGERS

*"There is nothing either good or bad but thinking makes it so."*

— WILLIAM SHAKESPEARE

When you're stuck in the overthinking cycle, it can be hard to take a step back and consider what's causing you to overthink so much in the first place. Not knowing what's causing your overthinking is actually contributing to your overthinking, which is why getting a handle on your triggers is so important. Once you gain an understanding of what's triggering your overthinking, you'll have a much easier time controlling — and even preventing — your overthinking habits.

Consider, for a moment, the situations in your life that are currently causing you stress. Perhaps you work in a fast-paced environment, or your landlord decided to increase the price of rent. Maybe you're going through a breakup, or a family member has fallen ill. You may feel like your life has gotten chaotic for a combination of reasons, and this is causing you to think too much about what you don't have control over. Like a pressure cooker, you're about to boil over. You've gotten overwhelmed by everything life has thrown at you, and you're not sure what to do about it.

A friend of mine (who's admittedly a bit of a perfectionist) went through a particularly rough time last year. The good things in his life — his job, his relationship, and his health — were coming apart at the seams. It made him feel like things were never as stable as he thought they were, and that thought alone terrified him. "It's a disaster," he told me, utterly defeated. "Why is all of this happening?"

He began to lose sleep and developed a binge eating habit because he was so overwhelmed. His binge eating, he told me, was the one thing he had control over. Except, he didn't. It was actually — horrifyingly — out of his control, so much so that he had to attend an inpatient facility. He's thankfully doing much better now, but my point is this: the illusion of control is dangerous, and it can snowball faster than you think. In my friend's case, giving into the illusion of control changed his life in a way that was pretty unpleasant.

I'll discuss the illusion of control and other common overthinking triggers in more detail below. Just knowing about these triggers can drastically improve your ability to stop overthinking everything. If my friend had had this particular tool on hand, he might have been able to rein things in before they got as bad as they did. He might have been able to take a step back and think logically about what he was going through — meaning he could have addressed his stressors in a healthy way.

Due to the fact that your brain is working overtime when you're trapped in the overthinking cycle, it can be difficult to keep your thoughts organized. This, as you may have guessed, can make things feel a lot more overwhelming than they actually are. When you're feeling this way, there are a number of things you can do to let off some steam (as previously discussed). It can be especially helpful to know how to avoid feeling this way in the first place, however, which is why we're going to add a new tool to your tool belt in this chapter: understanding your triggers!

Before we dive in, I do want to reiterate the fact that it's okay to feel overwhelmed sometimes. Life is often overwhelming, and some feelings simply need to be felt. Identifying and understanding your triggers is not about avoiding your emotions. It's just a matter of understanding where your emotions are coming from so that you can more effectively address them.

If your typical reaction to stress is to start overthinking about the things you can't control, then that's rather unproductive, don't you think? Learning how to identify and deal with the things that trigger your unproductive thinking can eventually help you reframe your unhelpful beliefs — which is a key part of overcoming overthinking.

*Reflection question: How often am I triggered into overthinking? To what degree is it sabotaging my life?*

## What Triggers Your Overthinking?

Overthinking is a very stressful and personal experience. Everyone's different, which means most people will have different psychological triggers that stem from different past life events. Most overthinkers also have to deal with chemical imbalances, which are caused by disorders like anxiety and depression. What triggers your overthinking mainly depends on you, what you've experienced, and how your brain functions. For most people, their overthinking tendencies are triggered by a combination of things.

Young people often find themselves overthinking about money and the future, which is perfectly understandable. Most 25 to 35-year-olds are only just finding their footing, which can make life feel unstable. This is especially true in today's world, where a global pandemic continues to rage and the cost of living is through the roof. As a result of poor financial literacy, many young people have had to face the fact that they're losing more money than they're making. This is obviously stressful, and it can send one into an overthinking spiral about their future.

Most of the time, a person's unhappiness stems from not being able to achieve their goals due to circumstances outside of their control. This is where overthinking often starts. If you can't afford rent at your apartment because the landlord raised the price, how are you ever going to afford a house one day? If you'll never be able to afford a house, how are you going to raise the big, happy family you've always dreamed of? Are you noticing what big jumps these are? Do you see how overthinking can take you from "I can't afford rent" to "I'll never raise a family" in the blink of an eye?

Obviously, not being able to afford rent in your mid-twenties does not immediately mean you'll never raise a family. That's just not logical, and the two things don't really have anything to do with each other. Also, just as a side note, you can raise a perfectly happy family in an apartment. Overthinkers tend to have such specific plans in mind that they're unable to make room for other possibilities. This kind of tunnel vision can be quite bad for your mental health. It can actually block you from achieving happiness. That's why it's a good idea to learn how to identify when you're experiencing tunnel vision about your future, as well as determine *why* you're having tunnel vision in the first place.

The same goes for overthinking. Overthinking is, in part, what gives most people tunnel vision. When you learn how to stop overthinking about your future (and anything else that stresses you out), you'll be able to loosen up and see things in a brand-new light. Let's go over some of the main psychological reasons you over-think everything below. Again, being aware of these triggers should prove to be a useful tool, so you'll defi-nitely want to keep them in mind!

### Childhood Learning

Unsurprisingly, overthinking is oftentimes a habit left over from childhood. This makes sense, considering the fact that overthinking tends to be a trauma response for a lot of people. When you were a kid, things might have been scary or stressful at home, and the only way you knew how to combat that stress was by worrying and overthinking about the situation at hand. For example, when my friend's dad was growing up, his alcoholic stepfather was abusive toward his wife and kids. Because of this, my friend's dad spent much of his childhood walking on eggshells. He would worry obsessively about his mom and younger siblings, and do things like clean up the house before his stepdad got home from work to prevent his mother from getting abused.

Obviously, no kid should have to go through this, but these things do happen. Overthinkers are usually accustomed to having to be the glue that holds everything together, and this takes a toll on most people. My friend's dad is still dealing with the trauma he had to endure from his childhood, despite the fact he leads a pretty good life now. In his own family, he's the glue that holds everything together, and I believe he believes that's his role. After all, that's what he learned when he was little. These things can become deeply ingrained in us, and we can transfer them to our kids as well — though we may not always be aware of it.

Understanding the roots of your overthinking problem is important, but you've also got to gain an understanding of what is triggering your overthinking in the present. Overcoming overthinking is complicated, and facing your present is just as crucial as facing your past in this respect.

### The Illusion of Control

I've briefly touched on the illusion of control, and for good reason. This is a massive trigger that can be difficult to recognize for a lot of people. When you feel helpless, it's only natural to want to remedy your helplessness however you can. There's a certain amount of desperation overthinkers go through in an effort to alleviate their helplessness (or the helplessness of those around them). The problem is, this desperation only makes it more difficult to think clearly and rationally during stressful events.

Naturally, when someone we care about is going through a hard time, we want to help them. The feeling of not being able to help someone else can be even worse than the feeling of not being able to help yourself. Overthinking about how you can help someone despite your lack of control over a given situation can *feel* helpful, even if your worrying is actually doing more harm than good. Remember my friend's dad from earlier? Well, his mother, for example, used to fuss over his siblings and him for the smallest reasons, which in turn made things more stressful. He'd worry about the fact that they were causing her stress, which, on top of our other stressors, was a lot to deal with.

The fact that his mother had the illusion of control, however, made her feel like she was helping them.

Mothers in particular often feel inclined to "fix" things for other people. They especially want to fix things for their children, which is sweet, but it makes it more difficult for their children to face similar issues later in life. This is part of the reason people with overthinking tendencies struggle with conflict so much. Many young adults never learned how to properly deal with conflict as kids, and so they find themselves trapped in the cycle of overthinking when stressful situations come up.

## Perfectionism

It's relatively common for people with overthinking tendencies to be perfectionists. To put it simply, perfectionists thrive on the feeling of being perfect. This can be a trauma response, a symptom of Obsessive Compulsive Disorder, or just another personality trait. Many overthinkers are perfectionists for a number of different reasons. For example, a person may have felt inadequate as a child or teenager, and so they're trying to make up for it as a young adult. Some overthinkers feel like they *need* every aspect of their life to be perfect, or else they won't be able to function properly. If this happens to be the case for you, it might be a good idea to speak to a therapist about it.

The perfectionism trigger can be linked to the illusion of control trigger. Needing things to be perfect in every aspect of your life stems from a need for control. If you've lacked control at any point in your life — as a kid or as a young adult — you're going to be hyper-aware of any semblance of control that's slipping through your fingers in the present and future. For perfectionists, the smallest inconvenience — the tiniest imperfection — can make them feel like everything is spinning out of control.

Honestly, one of the best things you can do for yourself as a perfectionist is to let go of control. This is easier said than done, but it's certainly possible if you have the right tools and information on hand. Letting go of the need to control everything is a big part of overcoming your overthinking tendencies. It might be hard at first, but I promise: you'll be much happier after you let go of the things you can't control.

### The Illusion of Certainty

To be human is to be uncertain, and yet, we *despise* being uncertain. People with overthinking tendencies oftentimes deny their uncertainty because it's easier than facing the possibility that something might not turn out the way they want it to. For example, let's say you have an interview coming up for a job you've always wanted. You might tell yourself: "I'm going to get this job," without leaving room for the possibility that you won't. Of course, it's good to be confident and optimistic to an extent. To fully deny the possibility of a bad outcome, though, is a good way to get your hopes up.

Now, if you've spent a lot of time preparing for this job interview, you have a right to be confident. It's basically a matter of finding a healthy balance. You don't want to tell yourself that you'll definitely succeed, but you don't want to convince yourself that you're going to fail, either. Either mindset can send you into the overthinking cycle when brought to the extreme, which can cause you to lose your focus. Expect the best but prepare for the worst. Stay sharp, and stay balanced, and you'll be okay.

### Secondary Gain

The thing about overthinking is it can bring out sympathy and pity from the people around you, which can feel pretty nice. A lot of people with overthinking tendencies will seek out this source of sympathy without even realizing it. This can unfortunately sap people's energy, so it's not a good habit to get into if you can avoid it. The last thing you want is for your friends to think of you as an emotional vampire. The problem is, it can be hard for overthinkers to realize that they're feeding off the sympathy of others. Most fail to recognize that this slight secondary gain could actually be fueling their overthinking.

If you struggle with overthinking, it might be a good idea to examine the relationships in your life. Do you find yourself complaining about your life every time you get together with friends? Do you rope them into your cycle of overthinking? Of course, it's okay to vent about your life sometimes, but you won't be the best company if all you ever do is complain. Please understand that I'm not advocating for toxic positivity or anything like that. It's just that it's important to be mindful of how your overthinking affects the people around you.

### *Fear of Conflict*

People who are afraid of conflict and confrontations are usually really good at avoiding these things. This is especially true for overthinkers, as overthinkers are used to thinking their way out of certain situations (despite the fact that this oftentimes doesn't work very well). The problem is, you can't avoid most conflicts forever. Eventually, that problem at work or with your relationship is going to come to a boiling point and you're going to have to do something about it. Continuing to ignore such a problem is only going to make things worse.

Think about it this way: if your stove is on fire, you're not going to ignore it and hope the fire goes away on its own. You're going to grab your trusty fire extinguisher and put the fire out as fast as you can. You can also call the fire department, which could be equated to asking for help from a friend or a coworker if you feel like you can't deal with a certain conflict on your own. You shouldn't fully rely on other people to put out your fires for you, but it's certainly okay to ask for help if you're feeling overwhelmed.

### Overgeneralization

People who overthink everything have oftentimes been praised for their critical thinking skills — by teachers and parents alike. In many cases, thinking excessively has always worked for them. Perhaps you did well on a paper in college because you put a lot of thought into it, or maybe you came up with a solution to a problem at work after thinking about it for hours. Naturally, you'd get praised for this, which would reinforce overthinking behaviors. For people who've used overthinking as a tool their whole lives, it can be difficult to understand where overthinking actually becomes unhelpful.

Again, this has to do with control. When writing a paper for school or trying to solve a problem at work, you have some semblance of control. Therefore, it makes sense to use your thinking skills to figure things out. If you're waiting to hear back after a job interview, or your family member is sick, however, you won't have much control over the situation. This means over-thinking and panicking about these things won't be helpful. It will only make you and those around you feel more stressed out.

## Root Causes of Overthinking Self-Quiz

There are plenty of things that could be triggering your overthinking tendencies. This quiz should help you to gain a better understanding of what your triggers are, as well as help you figure out how to effectively combat these triggers. Using the table below, allocate a percentage to each of the following categories depending on how much you feel each category represents a root cause of your overthinking:

| Trigger | Percentage (%) |
|---|---|
| Stress | |
| Anxiety | |
| Unresolved past experiences and childhood learning | |
| Negative self-talk | |
| Boredom | |
| Depression | |
| The illusion of control | |
| The illusion of uncertainty | |
| Perfectionism | |
| Secondary gain | |
| Overgeneralization | |
| Fear of conflict | |

## How Do I Recognize and Release My Overthinking Triggers?

One of the main problems people with overthinking tendencies face is the inability to identify and appropriately cope with their overthinking triggers. It's all good and well to understand that you're probably being triggered by something when you find yourself in the cycle of overthinking, but this understanding won't do you much good if you don't know how to take action and head off your overthinking habit.

Achieving happiness and inner peace takes time and practice, but it's definitely possible if you're willing to put the effort in. By knowing what your triggers are, understanding the various signs that you are being triggered, and taking the correct actions to stop these triggers from getting to you, you can end the cycle of overthinking and learn how to address your stressors in a healthy way. Let's get into it, shall we?

## *Know Your Triggers*

While the most common triggers for overthinking are undoubtedly stress and anxiety, you don't necessarily want to chalk it all up to stress and anxiety and call it a day. By not considering all of the possible options, you're doing yourself a disservice. You might think: "well, stress and anxiety are treatable with medication and Cognitive Behavioral Therapy." This is true, but what if you're dealing with more than stress and anxiety? Moreover, what if your stress and anxiety are actually symptoms of a completely different overthinking trigger?

You shouldn't dive too deeply into "what ifs" as that can amplify the problem, but it is important to know and understand all of your possible triggers so that you can effectively acknowledge and combat them. If you realize that your fear of conflict, for example, is causing you to overthink a certain situation, it's important to recognize that as a specific trigger. That way, you can say: "I'm being triggered by this right now, but I don't have to let it overpower me."

## *Know the Signs That You Are Being Triggered*

Studies show that overthinking can cause you to experience mental health issues as well as physical health issues — such as stomachaches, headaches, and insomnia. These are actually fairly common physical signs of anxiety and stress. If you've ever gotten a tension headache during a stressful situation, that's probably why! When you're stressed out, your body releases cortisol, which can weaken your immune system. This can make you more prone to serious illnesses, so it's important to destress as quickly as you can when you find yourself overthinking.

When you get triggered into overthinking about something, you might start to feel like you're physically hot or like your heart rate is elevated. Your hands might clam up and your thoughts will start racing. You'll feel like the only way to get rid of your racing thoughts is to "think" them out, which means more mental gymnastics. When you notice yourself feeling this way, take a deep breath and ground yourself. Try chanting a mantra or splashing some cold water on your face. Keep in mind that everything is going to be okay, and that overthinking is unproductive.

## *Take Action to Head Off Your Overthinking Fast*

WE'VE ALREADY TALKED a little bit about practicing mindfulness to combat your overthinking tendencies. I'd just like to reiterate how important and helpful being mindful in stressful situations can be, especially if something is triggering you. Learning how to stay present in the moment, rather than stressing out about something you won't be able to control in the future, is honestly the key to maintaining your mental health and happiness.

When you feel like you're about to spiral into the endless overthinking cycle, take a deep breath and take a step back from the situation. If you need to, take a walk around the block or write your thoughts down in a journal. Most of the time, if something feels like the end of the world, it's really not. Try to keep things in perspective, and you won't feel so helpless. Remember: it's all going to be okay.

*Reflection question: What else can I choose to do, other than overthinking, that can distract me from the habit?*

## Understand How Your Core Beliefs Can Cause Overthinking

Your core beliefs are essentially what makes you who you are as a person. They inform how you see yourself and the world, and can have a significant impact on your judgment and decision-making skills. Some people — especially younger adults who have lost their way in life — don't know what they believe. A big part of life is figuring that out, but still, a lack of beliefs can make one feel rather unstable.

Some core beliefs can help you find your way. They determine the ways in which you interact with the world, and help you stick to your personal values. This is great, but not all core beliefs are created equal. In fact, most people have a mixture of good and bad core beliefs, and it can be hard to differentiate between them. Because a person's belief system is hardly ever black and white, "good" and "bad" might not be the best descriptors. For this reason, I'll refer to "bad" core beliefs as unhelpful core beliefs from this point forward.

People develop their core beliefs — both helpful and unhelpful — from a variety of sources throughout their lives. Unsurprisingly, nature vs. nurture plays a big role. Oftentimes, you'll learn your first core beliefs from your parents, and as you get older, those beliefs might change. Those who come from unloving homes often have to relearn and redefine their core beliefs once they get the opportunity to move out of their parent's house. This can be a confusing process, and it's often what produces overthinkers.

Changing up your belief system might be a scary thought, but it's possible through Cognitive Behavioral Therapy. This type of therapy focuses specifically on helping people connect their behaviors with their thoughts and feelings. It trains your brain to be able to identify unhelpful thoughts and beliefs you might have about the world, yourself, and those around you. CBT can be extremely beneficial for a person with an over-thinking habit, which I'll dive into next.

## How Do You Reframe and Shift Unhelpful Core Beliefs?

Let's take a look at a few examples of common core beliefs that could be considered helpful and positive. "I deserve to be loved," for instance, is a helpful core belief, as is something like "people are essentially kind," or "my hard work will eventually pay off." These beliefs are typically born from an optimistic frame of mind, but pessimists can learn to think this way, too. As previously mentioned, it's just a matter of retraining your brain.

A lot of people, especially those with overthinking tendencies, will be more familiar with unhelpful core beliefs like "I don't fit in," and "nobody likes me." These negative beliefs often stem from personal insecurities, which a person can honestly spend their whole lifetime overcoming. Unhelpful core beliefs, like unhelpful or unproductive thoughts, are also a product of fear. Like a turtle's shell, they're meant to protect you from harm. However, more often than not, these types of beliefs prevent you from fully living your life.

So, how do you go about reframing and shifting your unhelpful core beliefs? The process isn't going to be easy, but with patience and hard work, it's entirely possible to reframe your negative thinking. The first step in this process is to acknowledge your unhelpful core beliefs. Try not to think of your unhelpful beliefs as "true." After all, they're usually not based in reality. Simply acknowledge that you have these beliefs, and that they're unhelpful and unhealthy. Realize that these beliefs are holding you back from living your life, and that you have to power to change things for yourself.

If you're having a hard time identifying your core beliefs, I recommend trying Cognitive Behavioral Therapy. A good therapist will be able to help you differentiate between your helpful beliefs from your unhelpful beliefs. They will also likely give you a tool kit, which you can use to reframe your unhelpful core beliefs. You won't know until you try!

## Interactive Element

I want to give you an opportunity to practice identifying and reframing your unhelpful core beliefs below. Remember: core beliefs are *beliefs*, not facts. Just because you feel a certain way about something, that does not make it the absolute truth. Fill out the worksheets below, and see what you discover about yourself.

### Core Beliefs Worksheet 1

Complete the following statements. Rather than spending too long thinking about it, try to write the first thing that comes into your head:

*I am* _____.

*Other people* _____.

*The world is* _____.

In the box below, write about how these statements make you feel. What experiences shaped these beliefs? Is there someone in your life that holds similar views?

Consider this: do these beliefs still serve you? What are some core beliefs that would be more productive and positive? Using the space below, reframe these three beliefs to reflect how you'd prefer to be able to see yourself and the world:

*I am* _____.

*Other people* _____.

*The world is* _____.

Write about how you might interpret or react to a certain situation if you're viewing it through the lens of your new core beliefs:

*Core Beliefs Worksheet 2*

THE EXERCISE below is designed to help you identify your negative or unhelpful core beliefs. Keep in mind that unhelpful core beliefs typically center around worthlessness, unlovability, and helplessness. Tick each box that applies below:

- I am helpless
- I am not lovable
- I am vulnerable
- I am inferior
- I am unworthy
- I am stupid
- I am a burden

**Summary Box**

MOST OF THE time when you start overthinking, it's because you've been triggered by something. The most common overthinking triggers include perfectionism, the illusion of control, overgeneralization, fear of conflict, and the illusion of certainty. Determining the root causes of your overthinking tendencies is the first step in overcoming your overthinking. It's important to be able to recognize what is causing your overthinking so that you can put a stop to it before you begin to spiral. Your core beliefs also play a big role in your tendency to overthink things. These beliefs have become ingrained in you because of past experiences, and they can oftentimes be unhelpful. Thankfully, with Cognitive Behavioral Therapy, it's totally possible to reframe your unhelpful core beliefs.

## Segue

If you've ever broken a bad habit before, you know how challenging it can be. If you're willing to put the time and work in, however, you can eventually shift yourself away from your overthinking habit. In the next chapter, I'll go over how habits are formed and how they can be broken.

# 8

# BREAKING THE HABIT

*"Although difficult, change is always possible. What holds us back from making the changes we desire are our own limiting thoughts and actions."*

— SATSUKI

Have you ever had a bad habit that you just couldn't seem to break? Perhaps you chewed your fingernails when you were in high school, or maybe you picked your nose as a little kid. We all do it! I'm not here to judge. Most people develop habits like these because they're dealing with anxious or stressful feelings, and their bad habits (chewing their nails, picking their nose, etc.) are somewhat comforting. It's like Linus from *Peanuts* with his security blanket. He carries it around everywhere because it comforts him, despite people telling him he has an unhealthy attachment to it.

Overthinking, as you may have guessed, is a bad habit, too. Although it may bring you some semblance of comfort in times of anxiety, it's ultimately preventing you from living your life to the fullest. Now, considering the fact that Linus uses his security blanket as a catapult, a weapon, a Christmas pageant costume, a Christmas tree skirt, and who knows what else, I'm going to give you a less silly example of a bad habit that's hard to break: smoking cigarettes.

A friend of mine recently stopped smoking cigarettes after being a heavy chain smoker for several years. How did he do this, you might ask? Well, as a matter of fact, he read a book. This book helped him realize that smoking was a security blanket — an *addiction* — and that it wasn't actually doing anything for him. All smoking ever did was empty his wallet and destroy his body. It wasn't helping him. It was harming him. Once you realize that your overthinking habit is harming you, you should have very little trouble breaking it.

Remember: overthinking everything isn't actually doing anything for you. It's not soothing your anxiety. It's not opening up new solutions to your problems. It's just making you miserable. If you're anything like Lauren and me, you've probably used overthinking as a vice for most of your life. You're used to overthinking, and you feel like you do it naturally at this point. The thing is, though, all bad habits can be broken. You just have to want to change.

A lot of people don't think about the fact that overthinking is just another bad habit. It's not something that's talked about very often, which is too bad. If more people thought of overthinking as a bad habit, most would have an easier time breaking the cycle. Admittedly, overthinking is less tangible than other bad habits. It happens entirely inside your brain, whereas biting your fingernails is a tactile experience. It's also much harder to hide a nail-biting habit, meaning people are more likely to scold you for it.

It's also worth noting that habits can be quite complicated, especially when they turn into addictions. Most people with smoking addictions, for example, *know* that smoking is bad for them. The problem is, they simply don't care. Showing them pictures of black lungs isn't going to work because they still feel like they're getting something out of smoking. Most adults don't like to be told what to do either, *especially* addicts.

For this reason, if you want to break your overthinking habit, you've got to tell yourself what to do. You've got to keep in mind that you are the boss of yourself. Your thoughts do not own you, and you do not have to do their bidding. Learning how to question and carefully consider your thoughts takes time and effort, but it's definitely worth it. You're taking control of your life, and that's something to be excited about!

*Reflection question: What thoughts do I automatically/habitually think without really questioning them?*

## How Are Thought Habits Formed?

The human brain loves routines, repetition, and patterns. There's a reason people dislike change and enjoy solving puzzles. When we notice a pattern or abide by a comfortable routine, we feel happy because we have a sense of what is coming next. In the previous chapter, I discussed the illusion of uncertainty and how humans hate being uncertain. With routines and patterns, there's an utter lack of uncertainty, and most people take significant comfort in that.

Have you ever asked your parents about the state of the world? Perhaps you've heard them utter something like this in response: "that's just the way things are." I've always found it interesting that older adults never seem to question *why* things are the way they are. I also question why we continue to go along with "the way things are" when the way we're currently doing things doesn't work all that well for people. I suppose it's awfully complicated, but still — "that's just the way things are" is such a non-solution.

It's also entirely based on habitual thinking. People are used to the way things are, so why change them? Why risk being uncomfortable for even a short amount of time? It's hard to change a broken system, so you might as well be complacent. I promise I'm not trying to depress you. I'm just being frank. Hopefully, this example will help you consider the fact that you are in your own world. You have your own system, but that system isn't working right now. Are you going to change it, or are you going to be complacent? The choice is yours.

Habitual thinking is essentially automatic thinking. When you learn and reinforce certain behavioral patterns, these patterns get etched into your neural pathways. You grow accustomed to walking along these pathways, so much so that you inadvertently close yourself off from other opportunities. Instead of taking risks that could potentially change your life for the better, you take the same path you always do and deepen the groove. Consider this excerpt from Robert Frost's insightful poem, "The Road Not Taken":

> *"I shall be telling this with a sigh*
> *Somewhere ages and ages hence:*
> *Two roads diverged in a wood, and I—*

*I took the one less traveled by,*
*And that has made all the difference.*"

As human beings, we want to know where to go (physically and mentally). We're always looking for the easiest way to get from Point A to Point B — the way that we know by heart. The way we know is safe and certain. Sometimes, though, you just have to take a chance. Changing a certain thought habit is always a leap of faith, but it's often well worth it.

That said, you should keep in mind that it won't be easy. Changing a habit is a lot like changing the way you part your hair. You're going against the grain, and it will be uncomfortable for a while. It's important to remember that that's perfectly normal, and that your discomfort will eventually fade. Let's take a look at how you can start to replace your bad habits, shall we?

## To Replace a Bad Habit, You Can Try These Steps

Most habits start out as defense mechanisms. They typically stem from things your parents told you in order to keep you safe when you were little. For example, when my friend was growing up, he lived by the sea. His mom always told him: "never turn your back on the ocean," which is fantastic advice because the ocean is unpredictable. Now, as an adult, he never ever turns his back on the ocean when he goes to the beach. Perhaps this is just common sense, but for him, it feels habitual. It's like he can hear his mother's voice in his head, and his inner child abides by her advice.

That's an example of a healthy habit, but, like anyone else, I have my fair share of unhealthy habits as well. For instance, I dig my fingernails into my palms and clench my teeth when I'm feeling stressed out. Most of the time, I won't even notice I'm doing this. I'll look down at my hands after the moment has passed and see all of the little crescent-moon indentations in my skin and have headaches from clenching. I've been doing this since I was a kid, and the fact that I do it subconsciously makes it difficult to stop.

Perhaps you have the same or a similar habit, so let's use it as our unhealthy habit example. Now, if we're going to eventually change this bad habit (i.e. replace it with a healthy one), there are a few things we'll need to do. Keep in mind that the following steps can also be applied to changing an overthinking habit.

### Step One: Identify Your Triggers

CONSIDER what triggers you to perform your habitual rituals (i.e. overthinking, digging your fingernails into your palms, clenching your teeth, etc). Perhaps there's someone at work who just grinds your gears, or maybe being around too many people on public transportation is too overwhelming. Whatever your triggers are, recognizing and naming them can help significantly. You'll begin to associate your bad habits with your triggers, meaning you'll be more likely to notice yourself feeling compelled to perform a habitual ritual.

### Step Two: Find a Replacement Habit

Now that you're aware of your various triggers, you should have some control over the bad habit you're trying to change. Name your bad habit so that it's fresh in your mind. Say to yourself: "I typically react to stress by digging my fingernails into my palms, but I'm trying to stop doing that because it's unhealthy." Consider what you can do instead of digging your fingernails into your palms. Perhaps you can practice belly breathing when you're feeling nervous.

## Step Three: Plan and Prepare

IF YOU'RE GOING to change your habitual behaviors for the better, you're going to need to come up with a solid plan. Most habits become habits because we inadvertently attach some sort of reward to our habitual behaviors. For example, when you dig your fingernails into your palms, you feel a sense of relief and release. Similarly, when you overthink something, you might feel better because you're tricking yourself into thinking you're being proactive and productive (when you're actually not).

When replacing a bad habit with a healthy habit, it's important to keep this reward system in mind. Once you've figured out a healthy habit to replace your unhealthy habit with, you can decide how this particular habit will be rewarding for you. For example, you'll get the same release from belly breathing that you do from digging your fingernails into your palms. It's just a matter of rewiring your brain!

## Step Four: Create Accountability

One of the best things you can do for yourself when trying to kick an unhealthy habit is to ask for help. Find a friend or family member who's willing to be a support system for you, or join a support group for overthinkers!

I also recommend creating even more accountability for yourself by tracking your progress in a journal. Writing down your thoughts and feelings each day will help you stay organized as well as aid you in processing what you're going through.

### Step Five: Reward Yourself

Changing or replacing an unhealthy habit is hard work! Once you've succeeded in sticking to your new, healthy habit for an extended period of time, you should definitely reward yourself. This can also create a good incentive for you to stick to your good habits. For example, you can tell yourself that you get to order pizza at the end of the week if you continue to follow your new habit. Of course, you shouldn't let pizza as a reward become a *new* unhealthy habit. Moderation is key when it comes to rewards.

### Step Six: Be Patient and Persistent

Change doesn't happen right away. I've seen way too many people get frustrated because they weren't able to kick their bad habits within a few days of attempting to do so. You've got to keep in mind that replacing your bad habits with healthy habits is going to take a considerable amount of grit and determination. It's also important to accept the fact that setbacks happen. Your habits are deeply ingrained, and you'll probably find yourself slipping up once or twice in times of stress. Don't give up! Have compassion for yourself and reflect on how you can do better next time.

## Practicing Self-Compassion

When you're in the process of changing an unhealthy habit, it's important to practice self-compassion. When others are going through something difficult, you typically show them empathy and compassion for their struggles, right? Perhaps you even take care of them for a short time if you love them very much. Well, it's important to show yourself that love and care as well! Overthinkers are highly sensitive and are oftentimes too hard on themselves. Perhaps this is something you've noticed about yourself in the past.

In Chapter 2, we did a deep dive into faulty cognition, which is essentially the concept of experiencing thoughts and feelings that aren't true. It's incredibly common for overthinkers to imagine problems where there really are none. For example, someone with an overthinking habit might feel like their friends are talking about them behind their back when that's actually not what's going on at all. Overthinkers may experience faulty cognition for several reasons, including trauma and past life events.

Those who have issues with faulty cognition tend to inadvertently create unhealthy coping mechanisms, such as avoiding other people or even lashing out at their loved ones. Most overthinkers are somewhat blinded by their faulty cognition, so it's hard for them to see that their coping mechanisms may be harmful to those around them. It also may be difficult for a highly sensitive overthinker to acknowledge that some of their coping mechanisms are unhealthy.

### *How to Practice Self-Compassion*

When you feel like you're overthinking something (i.e. experiencing a faulty cognitive bias), take a deep breath and consider this: you're not a mind reader. Let's say, for example, you feel like your two best friends are talking smack about you behind your back. Ask yourself why you feel this way. What exactly is triggering this thought process? If you really can't get it off your mind, ask your friends if they actually have been talking about you behind your back. Yes, there's always the possibility that they won't tell the truth, but if that's the case, they're not really your friends.

It's also important to keep in mind that everyone is going through their own stuff. Most of the time, the people around you aren't paying you any mind because they're too busy worrying about what other people are thinking or saying about them. Every single person in the world is living a life that is as complex and intricate as your own. Keep things in perspective and focus on yourself. I promise, you'll be just fine.

Like most things, having compassion for yourself takes time and plenty of practice. In part, practicing self-compassion involves reframing your negative core beliefs, which we touched on in Chapter 7. Learning about and practicing mindfulness can also make it easier for you to have compassion for yourself. Those who regularly practice self-love and self-care weren't born knowing how to do that. Through meditation and mindfulness, though, they figured out how to have self-compassion and live happier lives — and you can too!

## How Mindfulness Can Help You Master Your Mind, Body, and Life

There's nothing worse than feeling like you don't have control over your own mind. This lack of control is what makes being an overthinker scary at times. Nobody enjoys feeling like their thoughts are spiraling out of control! That's why learning how to gain control over your mind is so important. When you have a clear and confident mindset, you can tackle anything life throws at you. How does one develop a clear and confident mindset? A combination of strategies could work wonders, but the number one thing that is sure to improve your mindset is regularly practicing mindfulness.

Being mindful essentially involves staying calm, grounded, and clear-headed in stressful situations. You've got to realize that panicking during a stressful life event will only make matters worse. When you allow yourself to be mindful, you're basically accepting the fact that certain things are out of your control. Once you let go of control, you'll have a much easier time handling situations that typically trigger you into over-thinking. It's a matter of telling yourself: "This is out of my control right now, and that's okay. This is not the end of the world." Again, it's all about keeping things in perspective!

Now, I'm not saying you have to become a "zen master," but setting aside just fifteen minutes a day to practice mindfulness could make all the difference in your life. When you learn how to utilize mindfulness at work, home, and in other areas of your life, you might just find that the things you typically spend time and energy overthinking about never actually mattered that much in the first place.

Practicing mindfulness gives you a sense of your true wants and needs, meaning it'll allow you to effectively set boundaries with people who stress you out. Being mindful is also a key part of overcoming the various obstacles in your life. You'll be able to think about your problems — and the potential solutions to your problems — in a way that's actually constructive and productive. No more unhelpful thoughts or faulty cognitive biases throwing you off your game!

## What Can Help You Be More Mindful?

For most people, being mindful doesn't come naturally. This is perfectly okay, and it's the main reason mindfulness is something you should practice regularly. There are a number of ways you can practice mindfulness throughout your daily life, including meditating, focusing on the present moment, reflecting on what's happening in your life, and eliminating multitasking when life becomes too overwhelming. Let's go over these mindfulness methods in a bit more detail below:

## Meditation

CONTRARY TO POPULAR BELIEF, the point of meditation is not to become entirely undistracted and free of thought. You're not trying to reach some sort of destination when you meditate. You're simply exploring your mind and making yourself aware of every beautiful moment. Meditating is essentially the opposite of overthinking. Instead of overanalyzing your thoughts, you simply let them wash over you. Instead of letting your emotions get the best of you, you acknowledge and move past the emotions that you'd usually find upsetting. When you practice mindful meditation, you're asking yourself to suspend your judgments for a few minutes. You're allowing yourself to be curious about your mind, rather than being afraid of it. It takes practice, of course, but meditating frequently can truly work wonders!

## Reflection

Taking the time to reflect on your past and current life experiences is an excellent way to practice mindfulness. I'm not sure how many times I've recommended recording your thoughts and feelings in a journal throughout this book, but I suppose I can't recommend it enough! When you keep your thoughts and feelings bottled up inside, you risk propelling yourself into the vicious overthinking cycle. Write down your thoughts every now and then, and they won't seem so big and scary. Like meditating, learning how to properly reflect on your thoughts and emotions takes time and practice. Once you get the hang of it, though, you'll find that it's completely worth it.

**Focus on the Present Moment**

When you start stressing about your past or future, try bringing your focus back to the present moment. Remember: you can't change what happened in your past, nor can you control what's going to happen in your future. The present is what it's all about, and it's worth paying attention to. If you find yourself getting pulled into the overthinking cycle, use your five senses to form connections with what's happening around you. This will help you stay grounded and focused on what really matters.

**Stop Multitasking**

If you work a high-stress job, you're probably used to multitasking. Or, at the very least, you're used to your boss praising your coworkers for multitasking at the expense of their mental health. The fact of the matter is, the human brain isn't well-designed for multitasking.

You might have noticed that your computer has a hard time functioning properly when you have multiple tabs open at the same time. Your brain works in a very similar way. When you take on too much, it gets overloaded and chaos ensues. Although productivity is valued in our society, you won't be doing yourself any favors by attempting to multitask. Take things slowly, and you'll find that life will be more rewarding (and much more forgiving).

## Interactive Element

Now that you've learned about mindfulness and how to apply mindfulness to your everyday life, perhaps you'd like to practice a bit. Feel free to participate in the mindfulness exercises I've included below whenever you have the time to do so. If you're feeling confident and clear-headed, why not try the first exercise right now?

### *Mindfulness Exercise 1: The Raisin Exercise*

This exercise will work with any type of food, but I recommend using something small, tactile, and textured — such as a raisin. Hold the raisin in your hand, and pretend as if you've never seen a raisin before. This might feel a bit silly at first, but just bear with me! While holding the raisin, record what you notice about it. You can write in the spaces I've provided below if you wish to:

How does the raisin look? (don't just say "like a raisin.") _____.

How does the raisin feel? _____.

How does your skin respond when you manipulate it? _____.

How does it smell? _____.

How does it taste? _____.

This exercise should help you stay grounded and focused on the present. Pretty interesting, don't you think?

### Mindfulness Exercise 2: Mindful Seeing

This exercise requires a window with some kind of view. You can also step out into your back or front yard if you want to get some fresh air. Once you're comfortable, look at everything in your line of sight. What do you see? What do you notice? Don't just say "a squirrel" or "a garbage can." Consider the shapes, patterns, and colors of the objects around you. Pay attention to the wind, and how it makes the fallen leaves dance. Observe without being critical. Be aware of your surroundings, and just breathe. Do this until you feel more grounded and connected with the world around you.

## Summary Box

WITH A LITTLE TIME AND EFFORT, you'll find that breaking your overthinking habit is absolutely possible. Most of us are familiar with the feeling of getting trapped in a cycle, but here's what most people don't realize: you're not actually trapped! You have the power to take back your life. By practicing mindfulness and self-compassion, you can keep yourself from falling back into your old overthinking ways.

# CONCLUSION

*"You only have control over three things in your life, the thoughts you think, the images you visualize, and the actions you take."*

— JACK CANFIELD

Overthinking is a surprisingly common problem. People all over the world are plagued by overthinking tendencies, so it's a little bizarre that this particular issue isn't talked about more outside of the mental health and mindfulness communities. To make matters more difficult, people who aren't plagued by over-thinking tend to misunderstand overthinkers. If you've ever been called "dramatic" because of your overthinking habit, you know exactly what I'm talking about.

It's important to recognize that nobody is born an overthinker. Like Lauren and me, you likely developed your overthinking habit due to past trauma and undiagnosed or poorly-treated anxiety. The good news is, your overthinking habit is entirely manageable if you have the right tools on hand. Throughout this book, I've provided tools and information that you can arm yourself with when the going gets tough. You've got the power in your hands, and I believe that you can do this.

Pat yourself on the back, and consider all that you've learned throughout this process. First and foremost, understanding your overthinking habit is a crucial step in eventually overcoming it. You've also got to take your faulty cognitive biases into consideration, as these biases tend to be a common cause of overthinking for most people. Understanding your emotions and developing strategies for getting yourself "unstuck" when you feel overwhelmed is also essential.

Furthermore, if you want to overcome your overthinking habit, you're going to need to simplify your life. Oftentimes, we feel overwhelmed because we're trying to take on too much at one time. Sometimes, you can't avoid feeling overwhelmed, but you can remedy it. It's important to listen to your body and use one of the exercises listed in Chapter 6 to help yourself unwind when life feels too stressful. It's also a good idea to identify your triggers and learn how to diffuse your anxiety when you get triggered by something.

Lastly, practicing self-compassion and coming up with a plan to replace your overthinking habit is the key to overcoming it. Try to approach life with more mindfulness, and you'll find your happiness. It's right there, within your reach.

Now, to wrap things up, I'd like to share a success story with you: the story of a recovering overthinker named Claire Seeber. Claire, like many of us, spent way too much of her life worrying about what other people thought of her. She desperately wanted to feel like she was doing well in life — like she was successfully keeping her head above the surface — but this proved to be difficult because she was constantly overthinking everything.

Claire eventually realized that the time and energy she spent overthinking was actually preventing her from living her life. She started questioning her unhelpful thoughts. She asked herself: "why am I thinking about this, and is it worth investing this must energy?" She considered whether a particular worry would even be a blip on her radar in six months' time. She wondered: "what evidence do I have that this person actually has the opinion of me that I think they do?"

Claire accepted that overthinking was just a part of herself (as it is a part of all of us), but she understood that she had the power to control it. Her story shows that you don't have to be afraid of your overthinking habit. You simply have to ask yourself grounding questions, and rein it in a bit when you feel yourself starting to spiral. Claire is a self-declared "recovering overthinker," which is a wonderful way to put it. By being more mindful and taking the time to understand her overthinking habit, she eventually changed her life for the better — and you can too!

It's important to keep in mind that there's no "cure" for overthinking. As Claire states in her story, overthinking is simply a part of yourself. When you learn to accept and understand that part of yourself, you'll have a much easier time controlling it. You'll get to live the life you want to live on your own terms without worrying so much about everything. I hope you've enjoyed reading this book as much as I've enjoyed writing it. It would mean the world to me if you left a review, as that will further help people like you who are struggling with overthinking.

## Congratulations on finishing "Overcoming Overthinking!"

You've taken the first step towards a life free from anxiety, sleeplessness, indecision, and negative thoughts.

But before you close the book, I have a final request. Would you take a moment to leave an honest review of this book and its contents? Your review can help someone just like you who's seeking information but unsure where to look. It can be the difference between them continuing to suffer or finally finding the help they need.

In the middle of this book, we talked about the importance of helping others. And now, by leaving a review, you have the opportunity to do just that. Again, you can help:

- One more person conquer their anxiety
- One more person get a good night's sleep
- One more person make confident decisions
- One more person live a life free of negative thoughts

By helping others, you're also helping yourself. People who help others (with zero expectation) experience higher levels of fulfillment, live longer, and make more money.

So let's make a difference together. If you're on Audible, hit the three dots in the top right of your device, click rate & review, then leave a few sentences about the book with a 5-star rating. If you're reading on Kindle or an e-reader, scroll to the bottom of the book, then swipe up and it will automatically prompt a review. And if for some reason the functionality has changed, you can go to the book page on Amazon or wherever you purchased the book and leave a review there.

Thank you for taking the time to help others, and in turn, help yourself. You have the power to change someone's life with just a few words. Let's make it happen.

# OVERCOMING ANXIETY

A REFLECTIVE GUIDE FOR ADULTS TO
BREAK THE CYCLE OF WORRY AND TAKE
CONTROL OF YOUR MIND

# INTRODUCTION

You know the feeling. You're working hard at the office or cooking dinner for your family, just minding your own business, when all of a sudden your heart starts beating in your throat. Your hands clam up — they're shaking — and you're not sure why. You try to take a deep breath to calm yourself down, but the tightness in your chest only seems to get worse. "What is happening to me?" You wonder out loud. "*Why* is this happening to me?"

Did you know that anxiety is the most common mental illness there is? Around 30% of U.S. adults will experience some sort of anxiety-related disorder at some point in their lives. If you've been struggling or have ever struggled with an anxiety disorder, you're definitely not alone. Millions of people all over the world — including myself — have been there before. Anxiety is brutal, and there's no "quick fix" for it, but if you're willing to put the work in, it's absolutely possible for you to take back your life.

Take my good friend, Charles, for example. Charles is one of the kindest people I've ever met, but he's unfortunately struggled with anxiety for most of his life. Before he learned how to overcome his anxiety, it was a heavy burden that he carried around with him every single day. I could see how it affected him, both mentally and physically. He often had trouble eating and sleeping, and when we attended social events, he would bite his fingernails and wring his hands — both of which were anxious habits.

Charles knew he needed help, but he had no idea where to look. Anxiety had been plaguing him for years, and over time, he'd tried many different coping mechanisms, some of which weren't particularly healthy. He felt like he was drowning in his worries, and it was getting more and more difficult for him to keep his head above the surface.

When he thought all hope was lost, Charles happened to stumble upon the solution to his problem. It was as if a light bulb had gone off in his head. *This is it!* He thought to himself. *I'm going to be okay!* Finally, he had a clear path laid out in front of him, and following this path would eventually allow him to overcome his anxiety. Charles knew it wouldn't be easy, but he took it one step at a time, and slowly but surely began to see improvements.

Charles realized that the key to overcoming his anxiety was to confront it head-on. He recognized that he had to identify the root causes of his worries if he was going to successfully confront them, and from there came up with practical ways to manage his anxiety triggers. He learned how to prioritize self-care and began exercising regularly. He ate a healthy diet, and practiced mindful meditation, which helped to calm his mind.

Of course, the changes weren't immediate. Charles didn't walk the path of recovery without tripping over tree roots every now and then. He kept at it, though, and eventually, his anxiety began to subside. The world around him began to look a little brighter. He could finally breathe a little easier, and was able to do things his anxiety had previously prevented him from doing.

It can be hard to know where to turn or what to do when you're dealing with anxiety, but the solution to your problem may be closer than you think. By taking small steps every day and being persistent — just like Charles was — you can learn how to manage your anxiety and live a happier, healthier life. You have the power to overcome your worries. It all starts with taking that first step.

There are a lot of things that could be making you

anxious in your everyday life. The world is turbulent, and times are tough. You might be dealing with the anxiety that comes with growing up and moving out of your parents' house, or perhaps you've been run ragged by the corporate rat race and dread going to work every morning. At times, you might find yourself getting anxious for no identifiable reason. Your brain is seemingly getting hyperstimulated by something, but you're not sure what.

Anxiety mainly affects people between the ages of 18 to 29 and 30 to 44 (although, people of all ages can experience it). Millennials and Gen Z adults are significantly more anxious than previous generations, and women in particular are twice as likely to be diagnosed with an anxiety disorder. This has a lot to do with significant societal changes that have taken place. Millennials were forced to take menial jobs in 2008 when the Great Recession hit, and Gen Z adults were forced to put important milestones on hold when the Covid-19 pandemic wreaked havoc in 2020.

Women are more likely to experience anxiety than men due to a number of factors, such as hormone fluctuations, brain chemistry, sexism in the workplace, objectification, or domestic violence in relationships. Existing as a woman is, in general, more anxiety-inducing than existing as a man. My female friends have told me about the fear they experience while walking alone at night, which is something I've never had to worry about as a man.

They've shared stories about being harassed on public transportation, and being objectified at work. They deal with these things every day, and they somehow manage to turn the other cheek (or retaliate if it's safe to do so) and go about their lives. I admire their strength, but it's sad that these issues have become normalized. I'm not saying these things never happen to men — they do — but there's no denying that women are more likely to experience things like street harassment and objectification. It makes perfect sense that they're more anxious.

Anxiety is on the rise, and it has been for several years. Why, you might ask? Life in the U.S. has gotten more stressful for sure, but it's important to note that people may be more inclined to report their feelings of anxiety in this day and age. Mental health issues have become less stigmatized and better understood by the masses, so young people in particular will be more likely to admit when they're feeling anxious or depressed.

It's also important to keep in mind that simply experiencing anxious feelings does not equate to having an anxiety disorder. Everyone feels anxious sometimes, but those with Generalized Anxiety Disorder (GAD) will oftentimes experience anxiety that extends beyond logic and reason. For a person with GAD, the smallest stressor or inconvenience can feel like the end of the world.

If you feel as if you're in a constant state of distress or panic — like you've always got something biting at the back of your mind — I see you. If you get anxious about being anxious, just know that you're not alone. You might feel like your anxiety has been getting in the way of your relationships, as well as preventing you from forming new relationships with people you're interested in romantically or otherwise.

Perhaps your anxiety has started to significantly impact your sleeping and eating habits, meaning it has not only taken a toll on your mental health, but on your physical health as well. As with physical ailments that go untreated, mental ailments have a tendency to get worse over time, especially if you don't know what steps to take in order to help yourself. If you're tired of being at the mercy of your anxiety — if the panic attacks and sleepless nights have gotten to be too much — you're in the right place.

In this book, I'll be sharing the knowledge I've gathered over several years in hopes that it will provide you with the tools you need to confront your anxiety head-on. We'll be going over the symptoms of anxiety, as well as some common triggers and life changes that may have caused you to feel anxious in the past (and, retroactively, the future). I don't claim to have all the answers, and there aren't any "quick fixes" I can recommend. However, I can guarantee that you'll have a full tool belt by the time you reach the end of this book.

Like my friend, Charles, you can learn how to cope with your anxiety and live the life you were always meant to live. It won't be easy and it might take some time, but with enough persistence and determination, you'll get there. So, without further ado, let's get into what it takes to overcome anxiety.

# 1

## ANXIETY: FROM A TO WHY

*"Whatever is going to happen will happen, whether we worry or not."*

— ANA MONNAR

A nxiety is a beast with many faces. Think Koh The Face Stealer from the spirit world in the popular animated cartoon, *Avatar: The Last Airbender.* The multifaceted nature of anxiety can lead people to believe they're not actually experiencing it — even when they very much are. Anxiety can look how you might expect it to look (i.e. your mother pacing around the house and running her fingers through her hair while engaging in a stressful phone call), or it might hide itself within certain characteristics, such as perfectionism or obsession over minute details.

Sometimes, it can be difficult to differentiate between generalized anxiety and the feeling of simply being anxious. When my anxiety was at its worst, I tried absolutely everything to ignore it, assuming I was just anxious because of work or upcoming life events. I eventually realized, however, that it's not normal to dread going to work every day. You might feel slightly annoyed that you have to go to work some days, but I was losing sleep and vomiting every other morning due to my dread and anxiety surrounding work.

My job wasn't even particularly stressful at the time. I just dreaded it for *some* reason, despite the fact I actually sort of enjoyed it in the moment. This is just one example of how anxiety can make you think illogically and irrationally. If you've ever felt sick with worry before doing something you've done a million times before, or if you've ever said "no" to going out with your friends because the thought of being social made you anxious, you know what I'm talking about.

Whether you're aware of it or not, your anxiety is preventing you from living your life to the fullest. It masquerades as something that's keeping you safe, but in reality, anxiety is like an overprotective parent or partner. It's so focused on "keeping you safe" that it's actually preventing you from enjoying the things you used to enjoy. It's like in Disney's *Tangled*, when Mother Gothel tells Rapunzel that she must stay locked up in the tower "for her own safety." Rapunzel, with a little help, realizes that this isn't the case. She eventually leaves the tower and faces her fears — and you can too.

## What is Anxiety?

Anxiety is a sensation that's often accompanied by tense feelings, worried thoughts, and bodily changes such as elevated blood pressure and an increased heart rate. People with anxiety disorders like Generalized Anxiety Disorder (GAD) and Obsessive Compulsive Disorder (OCD) are typically plagued by intrusive thoughts or recurring worries. They might stay away from specific situations (i.e. going out to dinner with their friends or asking for a promotion at work) out of fear. They might also experience bodily side effects like sweating, trembling, nausea, and vomiting.

Although they're not the same thing, fear and anxiety are often used indiscriminately. It's important that you're able to differentiate between the two, however. To put it simply, fear is a proper, in-the-moment reaction to a clearly recognizable and specific danger, whereas anxiety is a long-lasting, widely focused, future-oriented response to a vague threat.

### What Causes Anxiety?

It's normal to occasionally feel anxious, especially in stressful situations. If you experience intense, excessive, and constant concern in ordinary situations, however, you may want to get evaluated for an anxiety disorder. Anxiety disorders usually involve recurrent bouts of extreme worry or panic that can peak in a matter of minutes. This is known as a "panic attack." It's important to note that not everyone with an anxiety disorder experiences panic attacks and not everyone who experiences panic attacks has an anxiety disorder by default.

These uncomfortable, hard-to-control, prolonged feelings of anxiety may impede your everyday activities and affect your personal relationships. Childhood or adolescence may be the first time symptoms appear, and oftentimes, these symptoms will last well into adulthood. The causes of anxiety can vary significantly. Whether or not you develop an anxiety disorder depends on your genetics, your past trauma, your physical health, your brain chemistry, the environment you're in, and the prejudices you face as a result of your race, gender, or sexuality. We'll go over this in a bit more detail later, so stick around!

### Risk Factors

As a human being, you've got to keep in mind that while you're strong, you're also delicate. Perhaps you've heard the Reza Farazmand quote: "Don't forget to drink water and get sunlight. You're basically a houseplant with more complicated emotions." Most human beings deal with an immense amount of stress throughout their daily lives, and some self-treat their stressed out feelings with drugs and/or alcohol. Let's briefly go over some of the risk factors — like drugs and alcohol — that are associated with anxiety. Again, we'll go over this in more detail later, so don't worry!

**Trauma**

Children who experienced neglect or witnessed upsetting events while growing up are more likely to eventually develop an anxiety-related disorder. Anxiety disorders can also manifest in adults who go through traumatic events.

**Stress Buildup**

Anxiety and various anxiety disorders can also be triggered by major life events (or smaller, stressful life events that have accumulated over time). It's like the steam that builds up in a pressure cooker. If that steam doesn't eventually get released, you're going to end up with rice all over your kitchen walls.

**Stress Due to Illness**

When you're experiencing a serious health problem, you may worry a lot about things like your future
and your treatment. This is quite normal, but if you're
sick with worry all the time due to being concerned or
stressed out about your illness, it could be an indication
of an underlying anxiety disorder.

**Other Mental Health Disorders**

Anxiety disorders — like OCD, for example — tend
to go hand-in-hand with other mental health disorders,
such as depression, PTSD, and ADHD. Your anxiety
may intensify your other mental health issues, or vice
versa.

**Genetics**

Anxiety disorders may run in your family. Sit down
with your mom, dad, or grandparents, and ask them if
they've ever struggled with an anxiety disorder. At least
one of your family members probably did or does, in
which case you can talk to them about your own experiences with anxiety (if they're open to that).

## Drugs or Alcohol

Many people use drugs and/or alcohol because they feel like it relieves their anxiety. However, the fact of the matter is, misuse of drugs and alcohol will usually make your anxiety symptoms worse.

### Anxiety Disorder... or Just Anxious?

At this point, you might be wondering: what exactly is the difference between anxiety and an anxiety disorder? Anxiety is a typical response to a stressful event or circumstance. It's essentially your body's internal alarm system. It warns you about situations that it perceives as dangerous, and prepares your body to either fight back, retreat, or stay very still. This is commonly known as the "fight, flight, or freeze" response.

An occasional bout of anxiety can be quite beneficial. For instance, it might inspire you to complete an assignment at work or carry pepper spray when walking alone at night. Even joyful occasions, like moving to a new town, or marking a significant milestone in your career can trigger anxiety. This is partly a result of the adrenaline that gets released into your system when you go through a major life event.

## Typical Anxiety

TYPICAL, everyday anxiety is almost always a response to stress. Most people feel anxious before giving a presentation at work or going out on a date with someone they like for the first time. When the stressor is over (i.e. you give a great presentation or have a nice time on your date), the anxiety goes away.

## Anxiety Disorders, However...

Those who suffer from anxiety disorders typically still feel anxious even *after* whatever has been causing them stress ends or is removed from the scenario. Oftentimes, people with anxiety disorders feel like they can't control their worrying, and some will even get physically ill if their anxiety becomes particularly severe.

There are essentially two things that define an anxiety disorder. First of all, your anxiety must be out of proportion to the situation or situations that are causing you stress. Second of all, if your anxiety makes it difficult for you to function normally, this could be an indication that you're suffering from an anxiety disorder. Basically, if your anxiety is so severe that it's negatively impacting your quality of life, it may be time to get a professional evaluation.

## Different Types of Anxiety Disorders

Anxiety disorders are quite common and treatable, but this does not mean they are easy to cope with. Experiencing an anxiety disorder can be quite confusing and disorienting. Those who aren't sure what they're experiencing might fall deeper into a state of panic, further exacerbating their anxious feelings. There are several different types of anxiety disorders you should be aware of. Simply being in the know can help you identify certain signs and symptoms before they get worse.

### *Generalized Anxiety Disorder (GAD)*

Generalized Anxiety Disorder is one of the most commonly-experienced mental disorders in the world. It can alter your behavior as well as change the way you perceive the universe around you. Those with GAD typically experience restlessness, general unease, irritability, and self-doubt. Some GAD sufferers have trouble forming meaningful relationships and focusing on important tasks because their anxious feelings are holding them back.

## Panic Disorder

THE MAJORITY OF THE TIME, panic attacks start abruptly and without any sort of warning. If you have Panic Disorder, a panic attack may happen to you at any moment — whether you're driving, shopping, sleeping, or in the midst of an important conference call. You might experience panic episodes frequently or infrequently depending on several factors. Although there are many different types of panic attacks, symptoms (such as sweating, quivering, nausea, and an elevated heart rate) typically climax within a few minutes. After a panic attack, you might feel exhausted and emotionally drained.

## Phobias

A person with a specific phobia will feel intense, irrational dread toward a certain circumstance, a living thing, a location, or a particular item. When someone has a phobia, they typically plan their lives around steering clear of things they perceive as risky. The imagined danger is always larger than the perceived threat that the fear-causing factor actually poses. Agoraphobia, for example, is a very common and irrational phobia.

For those who don't know, Agoraphobia is the fear

of not being able to escape a certain situation or place. Examples include being away from home or being stuck in an airplane. Agoraphobia is frequently misinterpreted as the fear of wide open spaces, but it can also refer to being cooped up in a tiny area, like an elevator, or bus. Other common phobias include Claustrophobia (the fear of being in a confined space), Emetophobia (the fear of vomiting), and Arachnophobia (the fear of spiders).

### Social Anxiety Disorder

Feeling shy or uneasy under specific circumstances is not always a symptom of Social Anxiety Disorder. Various personality traits and life events can affect a person's social comfort levels. Some people are inherently reserved and others are more outgoing (i.e. extroversion and introversion). The fear, anxiety, and avoidance that come with Social Anxiety Disorder are different from normal anxiety or uncertainty because they can affect relationships, routines, work, school, and hobbies. The onset of Social Anxiety Disorder usually occurs during the teenage years, although it can also happen in younger children and adults as well.

## Separation Anxiety Disorder

IT CAN BE difficult for professionals to diagnose Separation Anxiety Disorder. Usually, a diagnosis can be made when the symptoms are excessive for the developmental stage that the person experiencing said symptoms is currently in. Separation Anxiety Disorder also tends to impair everyday functioning, unlike run-of-the-mill separation anxiety, which is not typically debilitating for most people who experience it.

The symptoms of Separation Anxiety Disorder may include extreme and ongoing anxiety about being away from home or loved ones, ongoing fear of losing a parent or another loved one due to sickness or disaster, and a constant fear of bad things happening, such as getting lost, abducted, or separated from your loved ones. Separation Anxiety Disorder typically stems from past trauma surrounding abandonment.

## Post-Traumatic Stress Disorder (PTSD)

The first signs of Post-Traumatic Stress Disorder may emerge about one month after a traumatic incident takes place, however, some symptoms may take years to fully manifest. Oftentimes, the symptoms of PTSD (recurrent and unwanted distressing memories, night-mares, emotional turmoil, and avoidance of situations that are reminiscent of past trauma) can bring on significant issues in social, professional, and romantic interactions. Intrusive memories, avoidance, negative thought patterns, and changes in bodily and psychological responses are the four main categories professionals use to diagnose PTSD.

## *Acute Stress Disorder*

Some people may experience Acute Stress Disorder in the days and weeks following a stressful event. Within a month of said event, Acute Stress Disorder might manifest in full (much like PTSD). It usually lasts for a minimum of three days or a maximum of one month. Acute Stress Disorder patients typically exhibit symptoms resembling those of Post-Traumatic Stress Disorder.

## *Obsessive-Compulsive Disorder (OCD)*

OCD is characterized by a pattern of unwanted thoughts and worries (obsessions) that may cause the OCD sufferer to engage in repeated behaviors (compulsions). These compulsive thoughts and behaviors can disrupt everyday life and cause severe anguish. Those who suffer from OCD might try to suppress or disregard their obsessions and compulsions, but doing so tends to make them feel more anxious and upset. Because of this, many OCD sufferers become compelled to engage in obsessive behaviors in an effort to reduce their tension and anxiety. Despite attempts to disregard bothersome impulses or desires, these impulses often linger until the OCD sufferer performs the ritualistic compulsion. As you can see, it's a vicious cycle.

### Adjustment Disorder

Adjustment Disorder is a temporary and common condition. It's also known as situational depression. An individual who displays an exaggerated response to a stressful or upsetting event will oftentimes be diagnosed with Adjustment Disorder. Adjustment Disorder can be caused by one singular incident (such as a painful divorce) or several separate events (such as work problems, financial issues, and health scares). These stressors can affect a single person, a household, or an entire community (think natural disasters, for example).

### Selective Mutism

Do you know someone who's able to talk freely and frequently at home, but freezes up when faced with social situations in public settings? A person with Selective Mutism experiences extreme anxiety in certain social situations and is unable to communicate in particular social settings (i.e. at work). In other contexts, like at home with family, people with Selective Mutism are usually able to talk comfortably and communicate well with those around them.

## Misconceptions About Anxiety

While anxiety is extremely common, it's also quite misunderstood. Plenty of misinformation has been spread about anxiety and anxiety disorders, which has made the stigma surrounding anxiety that much more harmful to those who experience it. You've probably already heard some of the misconceptions about anxiety I've listed below, but if you haven't, this is generally what the misinformed believe:

### *Anxiety Isn't an Actual Illness*

Yeah, and Covid-19 isn't an actual illness either! Just kidding. It totally is, and so is anxiety. Many people don't realize that anxiety disorders go far beyond the general worries people experience in their everyday lives. The Diagnostic and Statistical Manual for Mental Health, Fifth Edition (DSM-5) requires a specific set of symptoms to be present for at least six months in order for someone to be diagnosed with an anxiety disorder. A person suffering from an anxiety disorder may experience severe disability and distress in their everyday life.

### Anxiety is Just a Phase

If anyone's ever told you this, they're gaslighting you (unintentionally or otherwise). Certain circumstances or stages of life may cause a person's worry levels to rise or fall. A person with an anxiety disorder, however, might occasionally experience a small improvement in symptoms or be able to get back to some of their usual activities. This might give some the impression that their anxiety disorder is no longer present or that the symptoms are "gone." However, anxiety disorders can be persistent and long-lasting, and if they're not treated properly, symptoms will probably return.

### Panic Attacks Always Result in Fainting

No two people will experience a panic attack in exactly the same way. A panic attack can cause a variety of symptoms, including breathing problems and a racing pulse. Although these symptoms are uncommon during panic attacks, some people may pass out or puke, which can heighten the anxiety they're already experiencing. The fear of passing out can occasionally make panicky feelings worse. The act of actually fainting during a panic attack, however, is a very severe reaction, and it rarely happens.

## People With Anxiety Should Just Avoid Things That Make Them Anxious

This is known as avoidance, which is actually a common symptom of anxiety. Needless to say, stressful situations can be particularly unpleasant for someone who's suffering from an anxiety disorder. Life is full of stressful situations, and developing effective coping mechanisms to help yourself cope with your anxious feelings in these situations is an essential part of managing your anxiety. In other words, you shouldn't avoid the things that make you anxious... you should confront them head-on!

## It's Obvious When Someone Has an Anxiety Disorder

Contrary to popular belief, a lot of people are really, *really* good at hiding their anxiety. Most of the time, another person's anxiety will be completely invisible to you. This is especially true of people who suffer from high-functioning anxiety. On the other hand, some people might struggle to conceal their symptoms because they feel worried about others noticing or calling attention to them. It really just depends on the person.

### Breathing into a Paper Bag Prevents Hyperventilation

You've undoubtedly seen this on T.V. or in a movie. A person who's hyperventilating breathes into a paper bag and it helps to calm them down. Although breathing into a paper bag can serve as a visual aid for people who are hyperventilating, it can also limit your oxygen supply. This could end up making your anxiety worse, as you'll be even shorter of breath. You'll be much better suited doing some mindful breathing exercises in the open air.

### Medication Is the Only Way to Manage Anxiety

Anxiety disorders come in many different forms, which means treatment options can vary significantly. Typically, a combination of medication and Cognitive Behavior Therapy (CBT) is helpful for most people. However, taking medication is not the only way to treat anxiety. The most effective course of treatment for any given patient will rely on the nature and intensity of their anxiety disorder, as well as their unique circumstances and preferences.

**Anxiety Look-Alikes**

Again, anxiety has many faces. It also has many clones! Listed below are some health problems that professionals may misdiagnose as anxiety:

- Heart problems
- Endocrine issues
- Asthma
- Diabetes
- Hyperthyroidism
- Sleep apnea
- Adrenal dysfunction/ Adrenal insufficiency
- Irritable bowel syndrome (IBS)
- Electrolyte imbalance
- Neurological conditions
- Postural Orthostatic Tachycardia Syndrome (POTS)
- Inappropriate Sinus Tachycardia (IST)
- Lung diseases
- Fibromyalgia
- Endometriosis
- Lyme Disease
- Ankylosing Spondylitis (AS)
- Crohn's Disease
- Polycystic Ovarian Syndrome (PCOS)

If you feel like you've been misdiagnosed, it can't hurt to get a second opinion from a different doctor. Trust your gut and look out for yourself!

## Segue

As you can see, anxiety disorders come in a variety of shapes and sizes. Anxiety is the beast with many faces, and it can oftentimes be difficult to diagnose. The misconceptions surrounding anxiety don't make things any easier for anxiety sufferers either. However, it's important to remember that anxiety is treatable and all hope is not lost. In the next chapter, I'll dive deeper into anxiety and give you a chance to reflect on your past and current experiences with it. Remember: anxiety is a journey and this journey affects different people in different ways.

# 2

# THE "I" IN THE MIDDLE OF ANXIETY

*"How much pain has cost us the evils which have never happened."*

— THOMAS JEFFERSON

Can you remember the first time you experienced feeling anxious? Maybe you felt nervous and excited at the same time when you woke up on Christmas morning as a kid, or perhaps you used to get a stomachache before your sports competitions in high school. The latter describes my earliest and most memorable experience with severe anxiety. I ran cross country throughout high school and college, and I would always, *always* get sick right before a big race.

As I discussed in the previous chapter, anxiety takes many different forms. It doesn't always look how you expect it to look, and it doesn't always feel how you expect it to feel. Most of the time, telling yourself "I'm just nervous," or "it's just anxiety" doesn't make your anxiety go away (at least, in my experience). People with anxiety disorders, who literally *cannot* calm down just by taking logic and reason into account, might wonder what the heck is going on if they've never been properly diagnosed.

Whenever my friend, Charles, was dealing with a particularly brutal bout of anxiety, he would freeze up. When his girlfriend asked him what was wrong, he'd say: "I just need to stay perfectly still right now," and, like a statue in an earthquake, he would stand ramrod straight and tremble uncontrollably. Charles's girlfriend became concerned and started looking into some grounding exercises. *"Can you tell me five things you can see?"* She'd ask him. *"Can you tell me five things you can hear?"* This helped a little, but it was a bandaid, not a cure.

Charles needed to reflect on his journey and his experiences with anxiety if he was going to confront it head-on. Although he appreciated his friends and his girlfriend being there for him, he was ultimately the one who had to help himself — and he did! It may have taken him a lot of time and effort to overcome his anxiety, but based on how well he's doing today, he would definitely agree it was worth it.

One of the main things that helped Charles reflect on his anxiety journey was writing about it. He started carrying a small journal around with him everywhere, and when he had a spare moment, he would sit down and record his thoughts. If he had something on his mind — a past experience that made him anxious, or an upcoming future stressor — he would take the time to ask himself certain questions (i.e. "What was making me feel anxious in that particular situation?" "What is making me feel this way now?"). Doing this allowed Charles to take control of his own thoughts and confront his anxiety. It helped him better understand himself, which in turn helped him gain a deeper understanding of his anxious thoughts and feelings.

While engaging with this chapter, I'd like to invite you to dig deep. Consider your personal journey with anxiety. How old were you when you first started experiencing a lot of anxiety? What are some of the things that make you feel most anxious now that you're an adult? Identifying your triggers and putting in the work to understand them is an important step in the process of overcoming your anxiety. It certainly won't be a walk in the park, but it *will* be worth it.

## Common Symptoms of Anxiety

We've already gone over some common anxiety symptoms, but it can't hurt to reiterate. The more you understand about your anxiety, the more success you'll have while confronting it. For this reason, I'd like to delve into some lesser-known symptoms of anxiety as well. Plenty of people are familiar with symptoms like sweaty palms and a churning stomach, but most aren't aware of some of the rarer anxiety symptoms — such as excessive yawning, pins and needles, and depersonalization. Let's get into it, shall we?

### Physical Effects

When you're dealing with severe anxiety, it can sometimes feel like you're experiencing a major health issue. As I discussed previously, this is why anxiety sometimes gets misdiagnosed. The common physical effects of anxiety include nausea, dizziness, an increased heart rate, dry mouth, rapid breathing (also known as hyperventilation), shortness of breath, sweating (especially cold sweats), tingling hands and feet, trembling, tense muscles, pins and needles, feeling weak, insomnia, grinding your teeth, and gastrointestinal (GI) issues.

It can be quite a lot to deal with! Although, it's

important to note that most people with anxiety won't experience all of these symptoms at the same time. For example, you're more likely to grind your teeth at night while you're sleeping, and you might not experience rarer symptoms like pins and needles or tingling hands and feet at all. Some people with anxiety might burst into tears or groan as if they're in pain. Some panic attacks may require a trip to the emergency room or another type of medical intervention.

### Psychological Effect

When it comes to the psychological effects of anxiety, things get a bit more complicated. Most psychological effects are invisible to others, and are oftentimes misunderstood by health professionals who aren't well-versed in mental health. People with anxiety who are experiencing psychological symptoms will typically have a difficult time articulating these types of symptoms, especially in the midst of a panic attack. Some common psychological symptoms of anxiety include trouble concentrating, avoiding things that trigger anxiety, an inability to relax, having a sense of dread or feeling like something terrible will happen, feeling like the world is speeding up or slowing down, and worrying about anxiety itself.

People experiencing the psychological effects of

anxiety will often seek reassurance from other people, or worry that they're losing touch with reality. Most will fall into a depressed mood and ruminate on the bad things that have happened to them. Another, less common psychological symptom is depersonalization, which essentially means feeling disconnected from your mind and body. Derealization is a relatively rare symptom as well. It's described as the feeling of being disconnected from the world around you, which can be quite scary.

### Other Uncommon Symptoms of Anxiety

Many people associate the word "anxiety" with uneasiness, an inability to sit still, sweating, or an increased heart rate. While these symptoms are common, they are not the only indications that someone is experiencing anxiety. Some people may experience anxiety in unusual ways and may never end up experiencing the more prevalent symptoms of anxiety. Some of the more uncommon symptoms of anxiety include chest pain, fatigue, brain shivers or "zaps," hives or skin rashes, tinnitus (a phantom ringing in the ears), excessive yawning, jaw pain, perfectionism, indecisiveness, cold hands and feet, and circulation problems.

If you find yourself experiencing one of these symptoms, you may want to have a professional evaluate you for an anxiety disorder. These symptoms are problematic anyway, healthwise, so it might be a good idea to see a doctor anyway. Something you definitely *shouldn't* do is look up your symptoms on the internet. People with anxiety oftentimes feel compelled to do this out of desperation for an immediate answer, but there's a lot of misinformation out there. Googling your symptoms is likely to make you feel more anxious, so it's best to avoid doing that at all costs.

## How Your Anxiety Could Be Affecting You

As I've already discussed, anxiety is a perfectly normal response to stress. This response starts in the Amygdala, which is the area of your brain that transmits distress signals to the hypothalamus. Your body receives these signals, which triggers a "fight, flight, or freeze" response. Everyone responds to stressful situations differently (which, of course, is psychologically fascinating). The "fight, flight, or freeze" response is generally a good thing, but it can end up causing issues if your body "freezes" in a situation where you should have fought back.

If you suffer from an anxiety disorder, it's going to affect you differently than run-of-the-mill anxiety does. Long-term stress responses to anxiety can end up causing negative emotional and physical reactions in your body. In other words, anxiety takes more of a mental and physical toll than you might think. Let's take a closer look at how anxiety can impact and alter your various bodily and brain systems below:

### Central Nervous System

Your brain is a delicate and complicated organ. If you suffer from chronic anxiety, your brain is going to be releasing stress hormones far more often than it should. You may experience headaches, vertigo, and depressive symptoms more frequently as a result. Basically, when you're feeling anxious, your brain fills your central nervous system with hormones and chemicals meant to help you react to a specific danger. Long-term exposure to these hormones (mainly adrenaline and cortisol) can be detrimental to your physical and mental health.

### Cardiovascular System

Those with anxiety disorders oftentimes suffer from heart palpitations, an increased heart rate, and chest pain. When these symptoms occur, your body is under an immense amount of stress. It's essentially working really hard to pump adrenaline and cortisol into your system so that you can effectively deal with whatever your brain is perceiving as threatening. This may increase your risk of experiencing a heart attack, especially if you already have heart problems.

## Gastrointestinal System

Stomachaches, nausea, and vomiting are some of the most common symptoms anxiety patients experience. A lot of people will also experience a loss of appetite. Studies show that anxiety and irritable bowel syndrome (IBS) could be connected, which makes sense because anxiety negatively impacts your gastrointestinal system. If you're constantly having diarrhea or throwing up, your GI system will never have a chance to fully heal. So, if anxiety is what's causing you to have these symptoms, it's very important that you address it.

## Immune System

When your body is under too much stress, it can negatively affect your immune system. It's crucial that your immune system remains in good shape because it's what helps you fight off diseases and viruses that can make you very sick. A person with chronic stress and anxiety, however, will typically have a weakened immune system because their body never truly returns to its normal functioning. This unfortunately puts anxiety sufferers at risk of developing infections and illnesses more frequently.

## Respiratory System

Hyperventilation is common in some people who experience panic attacks. This can put a lot of stress on a person's respiratory system, and if you have a condition like Chronic Obstructive Pulmonary Disease (COPD), the rapid breathing that comes with anxiety can make your symptoms much worse. This can sometimes result in hospitalization or a trip to the emergency room.

## Tips to Help You Identify Your Triggers

Most of the time, your anxiety is being triggered by something — whether you're aware of it or not. It can be difficult to identify your specific triggers, especially considering the fact that there could be a lot going on (in your surroundings and in your head) whilst you're experiencing anxious feelings or a panic attack. This, in and of itself, could be an anxiety trigger for you. When it comes to overcoming anxiety, identifying and understanding your triggers is an incredibly important step. If you're not sure where to start, don't worry. That's why I'm here!

### *Learn the Original Root of Your Anxiety*

Pinpointing the original root of your anxiety can be tricky. It might be beneficial for you to seek guidance from a therapist, as they should be able to help you access memories that are buried deep within you. Before you start digging for the root of your anxiety, though, you're going to want to manage your anxiety symptoms. If you're currently feeling anxious, try placing one hand on your chest and the other on your belly. As you breathe in and out, pay attention to when each of your hands goes up and down. You can do this standing up, sitting down, or lying on your bed.

From there, I suggest sitting in a comfortable position with your journal in front of you. Start writing about your past experiences with anxiety, and identify the moment or moments that you believe are continuing to contribute to your anxiety today. Try to dig deep. Consider your childhood and your teenagehood. A lot happens while you're growing up, and it's surprisingly easy to suppress negative memories as an adult. As you're writing, try to identify what you're truly afraid of as well as why you're afraid of it. This should help you figure a few things out!

*Think Back to What Triggered You in the Past*

ALTHOUGH THIS PROCESS might be unpleasant, it's completely necessary. Remember, you can always have a therapist walk you through this process if it makes you feel uncomfortable to do it on your own. Identifying your past triggers is also a crucial part of PTSD treatment, and hey, your anxiety could very well be intensifying possible PTSD symptoms (or vice versa). That said, it's important to remember that PTSD isn't always a result of a big traumatic event. Some people experience PTSD symptoms as a result of the build-up of small traumas that have shattered certain beliefs they once held dear.

*Look into Your Home Life*

Childhood is a particularly delicate stage of life. You're forming your sense of self and developing what will later become your core beliefs during this time. Although exploring your childhood and past home life can be emotionally draining, it's incredibly important. Keep in mind that looking back and reflecting on your home life isn't about blaming your parents, yourself, or the town you grew up in. It's about acknowledging the fact that your loved ones probably did their best with what they had, all things considered. In your journal, respond to the following questions in regard to your childhood and home life:

- What were my relationships like with my family members?
- Were there times that I felt ignored, shamed, punished, ridiculed, or afraid?
- Did I ever feel like I wasn't good enough?
- Did I ever feel like it wasn't okay to express myself?

### Consider Your Habits

Did you know that certain bad habits can trigger anxiety in some people? This is more common than you might think. Habits like drinking, smoking, and avoiding conflict can actually make your anxiety worse. It can be difficult for some to identify which habits could be contributing to their anxiety, but reflecting can work wonders. In your journal, reflect on the following questions. As you're writing, remember to take note of when your anxiety usually happens, where it happens, and how long your symptoms last:

- Has my anxiety (of the intensity of my anxiety) increased recently?
- Have my habits changed recently?

- How are my sleep habits?
- Have I been drinking or smoking more? How do I usually feel after drinking or smoking?

### List Your Fears

This can be a great way to pinpoint some of the things that are continuously triggering your anxious feelings. Try not to think too hard about it. Just write down the first things that come to mind. While writing, try not to judge yourself based on your fears. Everyone is afraid of something, and facing your fears is totally possible (especially if you identify them first).

### Pinpoint Patterns

Confronting your anxiety is like playing an elaborate game of connect-the-dots. In order to effectively overcome your anxiety, you're going to need to obtain a sense of understanding about yourself (i.e. how and why you operate the way you do). Pinpointing your anxiety patterns can be an excellent way to identify and understand the ways in which anxiety has impacted your life. In your journal, respond to the following questions:

- How long has it been since I felt differently (i.e. less anxious) than I do now?
- What has changed in my life over the past 3-6 months? How much has changed in a year?
- Were there other times in my life when I've felt anxious, but the situation was different?
- If yes, what happened? Is there a common thread between these situations?

### Consider Therapy

There's a lot of social stigma surrounding therapy, but in reality, there's absolutely nothing wrong with going to see a therapist when you need help managing your emotions. A therapist is a trained professional, and their job is not to judge you. Everyone could benefit from talking to a therapist sometimes, but weekly or bi-weekly therapy might be ideal if you're really struggling.

### Be Honest With Yourself (But Be Kind to Yourself)

Facing your fears and anxiety triggers is no easy task. Trust me, I get it. Although it might be hard, being honest with yourself and the people you confide in (i.e. your therapist, your friends, your family, etc) is one of the best things you can do to help yourself overcome your anxiety issues. If you can't be honest with yourself, you won't be able to get to the root of what's been causing your problems in the first place.

You should also, of course, be kind to yourself. Identifying your triggers can cause quite a bit of mental strain, so it's important to take breaks every now and then. Don't be too hard on yourself, either. It's fairly common for people with anxiety to ruminate on their past errors and experiences, but this is ultimately not productive. Practice self-compassion and be mindful of those around you. Take a deep breath, and surround yourself with love. You deserve it!

## Segue

The symptoms of anxiety are plentiful, and some symptoms in particular can be rather difficult to deal with. Identifying and understanding your symptoms can be quite helpful, as can identifying and understanding your triggers. In the next chapter, I'll go over some of the main anxiety triggers adults experience, as well as what you can do to combat these triggers.

# 3

# TRIGGER 1: WHEN LIFE THROWS YOU CURVEBALLS…

*"Life is 10% of what you experience and 90% of how you respond to it."*

— DOROTHY M. NEDDERMEYER

When you start to feel anxious, it's usually because you're being triggered by something. You may not be aware of it at first, but the trigger is there, lurking beneath the things that tend to pile up in the forefront of your mind: money, family, your physical health, and work. Chances are, you've become so accustomed to carrying these weights on your shoulders that you've stopped noticing how heavy they are. Even if everything is going relatively well with work, your family life, your health, and your financials, it's a lot to balance — and this balancing act itself can be stressful.

If you're suffering from an anxiety disorder, it can feel like the end of the world when one single thing goes wrong. My friend, Charles, could tell you this first-hand. When he was in his mid-twenties, everything was going swimmingly with his job, his relationship, and his physical health. He had gotten a promotion recently, and was thinking about proposing to his then-girl-friend. Obviously, he was over the moon that things were going so well for him, but an anxious thought lingered at the back of his mind at all times: "Okay, so when is the bad thing going to happen? When is all of this going to fall apart?"

People with anxiety tend to have a heightened sense of how fragile human life is. There's this constant fear that everything is going to come crashing down all at once. Perhaps you've felt this fear before. I know I have. When a person with anxiety gets triggered by a stressful life event, or even something small — like turning in an assignment a few hours late at work — their anxiety will often snowball. It will get very big very fast, which usually makes the anxiety-sufferer feel even more over-whelmed.

Charles, like many people with anxiety, developed an unhealthy coping mechanism, which likely coincided with or caused his depressed feelings. Instead of enjoying all of the good things in his life, he obsessed about when everything was going to turn sour. He anticipated things turning sour because in his eyes "they always did." He felt that his obsessive anticipation gave him relief from his anxiety because "if you anticipate that bad things will happen to you, you won't be surprised when they do."

It took him a long time to figure out that this was not a very good way to live. This coping mechanism gave him the illusion of control, but in reality, his anxiety still had control over him. Despite the fact that most things in his life were going well, Charles was miserable. "It was almost like I didn't know how to enjoy things," he would tell me later, once he started to figure himself out. "My brain wouldn't let me."

What eventually helped Charles help himself was this: he identified his triggers, and learned how to manage them effectively. In this chapter, I'll be going over a few of the main stressors that tend to trigger people with anxiety disorders. This should help you gain a deeper understanding of how these various life challenges are affecting you — as well as what you can do to help yourself when you're feeling anxious in the midst of life's many curveballs.

## Money Problems

In this day and age, a lot of people feel like they're working more than ever, yet somehow they're still losing money. This is the result of late-stage capitalism mixed with poor financial literacy. Young people, in particular, were never taught how to properly manage their finances, which means the majority of them have developed some rather unhealthy spending habits. Inflation is a very real thing as well, and it's something that's been causing almost everyone immense stress — especially considering the current cost of living.

### *What It Can Feel Like*

A number of factors can trigger financial anxiety. Oftentimes, it's not just about lacking money. People with financial anxiety frequently worry about their bills. They may be reluctant to check their bank accounts or deal with anything related to money at all, for that matter. Although financial anxiety might seem normal (everyone worries about money once in a while), it's just as serious as other types of anxiety. Financial anxiety can cause physical health problems, such as difficulty sleeping, trouble concentrating, and a loss of appetite. It's definitely not something you want to ignore.

### What It Can Look Like

#### Overspending

You'd think that being concerned about money would make you more inclined to save it, but shopping can actually give you relief from your anxiety, so many people use it as a coping mechanism. The problem is, spending more money in an attempt to find relief will just make your money situation worse.

#### Hoarding

Excessive spending can oftentimes result in hoarding. People tend to seek solace in material possessions, and because of this, some will end up buying a lot of useless things without ever throwing anything away. This hoarding behavior is usually somewhat obsessive, and although it can be calming in the short term, it's not particularly healthy.

### Fear of Spending

Being overly thrifty is essentially the opposite of hoarding. Saving your money in an exceptionally obsessive way could prevent you from taking vacations or providing yourself with a comfortable living situation. Some people who are afraid of spending might skip out on things like medical treatment and necessary car maintenance. This form of anxiety can also affect those who overwork or work compulsively in order to increase their income.

### Uncontrollable Finances

Those who experience financial anxiety might be uncomfortable making and saving money. This can have a devastating effect on things like retirement planning, or saving up for a future home. This form of financial anxiety can make it impossible for anxiety sufferers to budget properly, which, of course, only serves to make their financial anxiety worse.

### Depression

A person with financial anxiety will often experience depressed feelings about the world around them. They might feel like nothing ever goes right for them, money-wise, and that budgeting and saving are impossible due to things like inflation and capitalism. While inflation and capitalism do make things difficult for most people, these things do not make budgeting and saving *impossible*. Those with financial anxiety will have a hard time realizing this, however.

### *What Can You Do?*

IF YOU'RE STRUGGLING with financial anxiety, just know that you're not alone. Plenty of people all over the world are currently dealing with this form of anxiety, and the triggers — prices going up, budget cuts, expensive health scares, downsizing, etc — can be crushing and constant. Thankfully, there are a number of things you can do if you've been feeling anxious about your finances. Let's go over some financial strategies that should help to alleviate some of the anxiety you've been experiencing below.

**Set Financial Goals**

If you're dealing with financial anxiety, one of the best things you can do for yourself is set some solid financial goals. Decide that you're going to save a certain amount of money by a specific date, and start setting it aside in a savings account or piggy bank. Even if you're only able to set aside $10 per month, that's still better than nothing. It's amazing how anxiety-relieving having some savings can be!

**Keep Track of Your Spending**

It can be difficult to keep track of your spending, especially with things like automatic payments for monthly subscriptions being a major factor. People with financial anxiety might not *want* to keep track of their spending because paying attention to that sort of thing can be anxiety-inducing. However, you're going to be much better off in the long run if you keep track of your spending habits and avoid spending too much money on things you don't really need. That way, you'll be able to save and eventually relieve your financial anxiety.

### Make a Financial Plan... and Stick to It

If you've been struggling with finances, the first thing you're going to want to do is identify your various financial problems and pain points. Are you attempting to live outside of your means? Do you have any monthly subscriptions — such as Netflix and Hulu — that you'd feel comfortable living without? Once you identify the source of what's been draining your money, you'll be able to come up with a financial plan and put that plan into action. Remember to monitor your progress, and don't get discouraged by setbacks. It's a marathon, not a sprint.

### Create a Budget

What are your monthly spending habits like? Do you always set aside money for things like rent and bills, or do you spend as you see fit and hope for the best? If it's the latter, don't worry. I've been there too, and I know how hard it can be to change your bad spending habits. The easiest way to do so is to create a weekly or monthly budget. Sit down and figure out how much money you're going to spend on your necessities (i.e. rent, food, bills, doctor's appointments, etc.) Then, you can determine how much of your budget you're going to contribute to your savings account, your emergency fund — and finally — things like takeout, clothes, and video games.

**Manage Your Debt**

It's difficult for most people to live a full life without accumulating some debt here and there. If you happen to have student debt or credit card debt looming over you, just know that there are ways to effectively manage this. It's important that you contribute a small part of your weekly or monthly budget to paying off your debts, as you don't want them to keep accumulating interest. If need be, you can create an extra source of income for yourself — such as dog walking or renting out an extra room in your house. This will help you save up enough money to eventually pay off your debts.

**Create an Emergency Fund**

There's nothing more stressful than not having enough money to pay for healthcare, house maintenance, or car maintenance when an emergency occurs. Emergencies can be scary, and they usually come out of nowhere. You never know when you're going to have to rush your significant other to the emergency room or take your pet to the vet for emergency surgery. These things happen, but setting up an emergency fund will ensure that you'll be able to take care of the financial side of things when they do.

### Don't Compare Yourself to Others

It's perfectly natural to compare yourself to others, especially with the prevalence of social media and wealthy influencers showing off their luxurious lifestyles. It's very important, however, that you don't compare your life to the lives of people on social media. Most of the time, social media is a facade. People aren't going to share the *bad* parts of their lives on Instagram. They're only going to share the highlights. Chances are, they're struggling just as much as you are (even if that struggle isn't financial in nature).

## Grief

When you're grieving, it can oftentimes feel like you've lost all sense of control — which, of course, can feed your anxiety. The passing of a loved one is always stressful and sad. It's perfectly normal (and healthy) to grieve, but if you've been through insurmountable grief in your life, it has probably taken a toll on both your physical and mental health. Those who have lost someone dear to them will typically be reluctant to get close to someone else in the same way after the fact. Those with terminally ill parents or siblings may have a heightened sense of anxiety due to anticipatory grief.

The fear of losing a particular loved one may loom over them and cause them to feel on edge.

Grief is a huge, complicated emotion, and it's not something the average person can healthily deal with if they don't have a good support system. When I lost my best friend to cancer, I didn't know how to cope. The fact that the world kept moving forward after she was gone seemed absurd to me. It made me angry for a long time, and then, for even longer, it made me sad. She passed away almost a decade ago, and it *still* makes me sad. I've come to realize, though, that she would want me to accept her death and move on with my life. Of course, this is easier said than done. I'm probably always going to have a hole in my heart, but I'm learning how to patch it up. Slowly but surely.

I'm not telling you this story to make you sad, or to trigger you in any way. I just want you to know that you're not alone. One thing I've noticed about the topic of grief is that we don't talk about it enough. Talking about grief might be painful — especially for those who have lost someone — but it's an incredibly important part of the healing process. So, let's talk about it.

### What It Can Feel Like

Grief is a natural reaction to loss. It tends to go hand in hand with anxiety, especially in the early stages (i.e.

denial, anger, and bargaining). From there, one will typically slip into depression, which is the longest stage of grief for most people. The final stage of grief, as you may or may not know, is acceptance. It's important to keep in mind, however, that just because you've accepted the death of the person or pet you've been grieving, that doesn't mean you're done grieving forever. Anyone who's lost someone knows it's more complicated than that.

Those who are grieving might feel unsafe or like they don't have control in certain situations. They might start to feel anxious about their own health, or the health of their loved ones. Some people who are going through the cycle of grief might lash out at others, or avoid social situations. It's important to note that everyone experiences grief differently. You might feel numb after a loved one passes, or you might feel overwhelmed with emotion. That — in part — is what makes grief such a significant anxiety trigger.

### What It Can Look Like

#### Denial

For a person who's just lost someone, it can be difficult to face reality. Losing someone you love can be an extreme shock to the system, and it's only natural to feel like everything is slipping through your fingers all of a sudden. Those who have recently lost someone might stay in a state of denial for quite some time. It's a common coping mechanism, but it is oftentimes short-lived.

**Anger**

The next stage in the grief cycle is usually anger. After losing someone you love, it's normal to feel angry about the lack of control you have over the situation. You might feel like life isn't fair, and that the whole world is trash without that person in it. I know that's how I felt when I lost my friend. In this stage, you may lash out at others and burst into tears at random times. This stage can be difficult, but remember to breathe. This too shall pass.

**Bargaining**

In order to feel more in control of the situation, or to more effectively cope with your loss, you might attempt to bargain with the truth. This stage is similar to denial, although it's a bit more complicated. You may get nervous, irritable, and eventually depressed when you realize that some of the "what ifs" you've been entertaining wouldn't have prevented the loss from happening.

**Depression**

The depression stage is probably what most people think of when they think of grief. This stage tends to be quite long, and for a lot of people, it's the most difficult stage of grief to get through. When in the depression stage, you might experience bouts of intense sadness and isolate yourself from others. You may feel fearful about what's going to happen next, which, in turn, can amplify your anxiety.

**Acceptance**

Once you learn how to accept the reality of your loss, you'll be able to focus on healing. Acceptance is a leap of faith. It's a huge mountain to climb over, and a lot of people can't do it alone. The steps that follow the grieving process might make some people feel anxious because they know that they're going to be entering into a period of significant change. Some may feel like everything is changing too fast, and that they're not ready to let go quite yet. This is understandably anxiety-inducing, but coping mechanisms like attending talk therapy and practicing self-care can help.

*What Can You Do?*

Remember, the grieving process is normal and healthy — just so long as you have the tools to effectively manage your emotions once you've been through all of the stages of the grief cycle. It's possible for some people with anxiety to be diagnosed with prolonged grief disorder, which is essentially a complicated form of grief that takes an abnormally long time to go away.

This is relatively rare, and most of the time, it's a trauma response. However, it's still something to be aware of. Let's go over some strategies you can try out if you've been having a difficult time coping with your grief below.

### Make Space for Grief

The last thing you want to do is bottle up painful emotions. Although shoving your emotions under the rug may feel easier at first, it's ultimately going to make your anxiety and depression worse. Grief is your body's way of handling the unique stress that comes with losing a loved one, and it's healthy for you to experience the emotions that accompany it. I've mentioned, a few times now, the importance of confronting your anxiety head-on. Confronting your feelings of grief head-on is a big part of confronting your anxiety as a whole.

### Practice Self-Care

When you're going through a grieving period, it can be difficult to take proper care of yourself. This is especially true during the depression stage. You might lose your appetite or feel unable to practice good personal hygiene during this time. Although it might be hard, practicing self-care can make you feel a whole lot better. Even just taking a shower and putting on some clean clothes can work wonders. Getting yourself outside and breathing in the fresh air might help as well.

### Write About Your Grief

If you're not sure how to process your grief, try writing about it. Writing can be a great way to organize your thoughts and emotions, and it's a fantastic form of self-expression, too. You might find it therapeutic to keep a journal and track your emotions throughout your grieving process. If you enjoy creative writing, you might gain some solace from writing a poem or a creative essay about the person you've lost. This would also be a wonderful way to pay homage to that person.

## Seek Out Support and Connection

Grief counseling can be exceptionally helpful. Sometimes, what a person going through the grief cycle needs most is someone to talk to. A good grief counselor will be able to help you manage your complicated emotions as well as provide you with effective coping tools. It's also a good idea to stay connected with your other loved ones. For example, if you and your friend both knew the person who passed away, your friend might be going through their own grieving process. Grieving together can be therapeutic in comparison to grieving alone, so don't be afraid to reach out to them.

## Severe Illness Diagnosis/Health Problems

Whether it's a chronic or life-threatening condition, like cancer, or a significant health event — like a stroke, heart attack, or immobilizing injury — getting diagnosed with a serious health problem can be incredibly disruptive and anxiety-inducing. Most major health problems seem to appear out of nowhere, and they can completely derail your life.

If you've been diagnosed with a serious health problem, you may feel paralyzed by shock or overwhelmed with the sense that you'll never be able to properly cope with your illness. Some might feel numb or emotionally exhausted, and some might respond with denial, anger, or bargaining (i.e. some might experience the five stages of grief). The inner turmoil you feel after getting a serious diagnosis might make it difficult for you to think clearly or perform your daily tasks at work. In some cases, being diagnosed with a chronic health problem can cause a person to develop depression or an anxiety disorder.

### What It Can Feel Like

Life changes are scary for a lot of people, and being diagnosed with a serious illness is one of the biggest life changes a person can go through. Those who are in this situation might worry about the future. They might grieve the loss of their old life, and be unable to look past the worst-case scenario. Some may worry about what will happen to their loved ones after they're gone, and some may become obsessed with death and the dying process. All of this, of course, can mess with your brain in a big way — so much so that it can contribute to the deterioration of your physical health.

### *What It Can Look Like*

PEOPLE WHO HAVE BEEN DIAGNOSED with a serious health problem may try to avoid thinking about death and dying at all costs. They might get dizzy, or experience panic attacks when they think about dying because the possibility of death has suddenly become all too real. Some people might become obsessive about requesting medical tests and going to doctor's appointments more often than they need to. They might become depressed, or feel frustrated with their situation — which is understandable. However, living out the rest of your days in a state of despair is not ideal, which is why I've listed some effective coping strategies below.

### *What Can You Do?*

#### Understand Your Condition

Gaining a deeper understanding of your condition may alleviate some of the fear and stress you're feeling about it. The more you understand something, the less scary it will seem. It's important that you ask your doctor questions and be patient with the pace of your treatment and recovery. Seek support from others when you need it, and be open to the changes that are about to happen in your life. Take a deep breath. The situation is not ideal, but you're going to have an easier time dealing with it if you learn to accept it.

### Explore Your Emotions

Participating in activities like making mind maps and journaling daily can help you explore and more effectively manage your emotions. Doing this can help you distinguish between your worries that are solvable and your worries that are unsolvable. Writing in a journal is also a great way to process your emotions. You'll have an easier time keeping track of your thoughts, which should help you figure out what you're really thinking and feeling about all of this.

### Pursue Activities That Bring You Joy

When you're dealing with a serious illness, it can be helpful to distract yourself. This might be a good time to pick up a hobby you've been neglecting for a long time — such as painting or bird watching. You may be inclined to learn something new, or you may gain a newfound appreciation for nature. Enjoy the little things, and spend time with the people you love most. Talk to others about your thoughts and emotions, and spread joy wherever you can. Take care of yourself and be responsible for your own happiness. Trust me. It'll help.

## Losing a Job

Losing your job can be extremely stressful. Your job is likely how you support yourself and your family. You know that without it you might not be able to do things like pay rent or put dinner on the table. Looking for a job can be equally as stressful, especially if you're scrambling to find work after getting downsized or replaced by an automated system. If you've lost your job recently, you might feel downtrodden and anxious about the future. You might be questioning your identity, which is a symptom that tends to accompany feeling powerless. Let's talk more about the unique stress that comes with losing a job below.

### *What It Can Feel Like*

Losing a job often comes with its own grieving process. You may miss the structure that work gave you, or feel a loss of control over the direction your life is headed. Some people going through unemployment will find themselves feeling hopeless and insecure after losing a job. They might feel betrayed by their employer, or they might blame *themselves* for losing their job in the first place — which is actually rather in line with the symptoms of anxiety and depression. You may feel even worse if the job loss *was* somehow your fault, but listen: everyone makes mistakes, and a lot of employers do not (for whatever reason) allow room for human error. Don't ruminate on it. That will only make things worse.

### What It Can Look Like

Those who are going through unemployment may experience physical symptoms due to the stress and anxiety they might be feeling. These symptoms may include depression, insomnia, back pain, headaches, and high blood pressure. Some might get into the habit of self-medicating with drugs or alcohol, and some might spend most of their days "sick in bed." Remember, losing a job comes with its own grieving process. It's perfectly natural to lose the will to take proper care of yourself for a little while, but this is a dangerous road to go down. Let's talk about what you can do if you've recently lost a job and are having a difficult time coping with the anxiety that comes with that.

### What Can You Do?

#### Face Your Feelings

If you've lost a job recently, you're probably experiencing a lot of complicated feelings. It's very important that you allow yourself to *feel* these feelings rather than bottle them up. Try not to beat yourself up about the job loss, and look for any silver linings in the situation. Perhaps you were unhappy in that position, anyway, and now you have the opportunity to find a better job. If you'd like to, you can write about your feelings in your journal. This will help you accept reality and avoid internalizing your feelings of rejection.

**Seek Out a Support System**

You shouldn't have to go through the stress of unemployment alone. Try to think of this as an opportunity to reconnect with old friends or open up to your family members. If you're feeling ready to find new employment, join a job club and network to create meaningful connections. Spend time with those you love most, and try to let go of the things you can't control. There's no sense in spending all of your time worrying about the future of your employment because that's not something you can control during all hours of the day. Take the time to relax with your friends and family. You deserve to do so.

**Find Other Ways to Define Yourself**

This might be a good time to pick up a new hobby or get back into something you enjoyed previously but haven't really had time to engage in because of work. Go on camping trips with your friends, and start writing that novel you've been putting off. Volunteer at your local humane society, and get into a new routine to keep yourself busy. As cheesy as it may sound, life is for the living. Just because you're unemployed, that doesn't mean you have to put your life on hold. Get out there, and live it to the fullest.

### Practice Radical Acceptance

Radical acceptance is all about accepting the fact that there are some things in your life that you can't control. It's okay to feel your feelings and grieve about losing a job, but ruminating on it ultimately isn't productive. The best thing you can do for yourself in this situation is accept your unemployment and move on. Once you're able to do this, you'll be able to search for a new job and get your life back on track.

### Segue

Life is full of unique challenges, and many of these challenges — particularly money problems, job loss, illness diagnosis, and grief — can trigger anxiety in a lot of people. Existing as a human being is difficult, but it's also beautiful. You have the power to be responsible for your own happiness and health, even when life throws you curveballs. In the next chapter, I'll discuss some of the anxiety triggers you may face in your everyday life — as well as some strategies to help you cope with these triggers.

# 4

# TRIGGER 2: WHEN LIFE JUST HAPPENS...

*"He who is not every day conquering some fear has not learned the secret of life."*

— RALPH WALDO EMERSON

While big life challenges, like losing a job or getting a serious health diagnosis, are almost always anxiety-inducing, there are a number of everyday life challenges that can be quite triggering for people with anxiety as well. Big anxiety triggers — like going to college or starting a new job — can branch off into a whole bunch of smaller triggers, such as having to live with a roommate for the first time or having to give a presentation at work. While these changes are exciting, they can also be quite nerve-wracking, especially for someone with an anxiety disorder. For some, the anxiety might outweigh the excitement, which may ruin the mood and prevent the anxiety sufferer from enjoying what should be an invigorating time in their life.

When Charles was a freshman in college, he found it nearly impossible to leave his dorm room for the first few weeks. Even going to the cafeteria felt like too much because of his social anxiety. He started spending money he didn't have on microwaveable meals and takeout just so he could avoid going to the cafeteria — where he was sure he'd be forced to sit alone around hundreds of people — which in his mind, was the absolute *worst*. Of course, this was his heightened sense of anxiety attempting to protect him from social rejection. His anxiety convinced him that it was better to be alone all by himself than to sit alone while surrounded by a bunch of strangers.

The problem with this logic is, if you never put yourself out there, strangers will continue to be strangers. Charles was introverted to an extreme, but he eventually realized that he was going to have to rip the bandaid off and make some friends. He started talking casually with people in his classes, and joined his school's rowing team, which made him feel like a part of a community. Suddenly, he had people to sit with in the cafeteria and friends to hang out with on the weekends. Making friends can take time for people with anxiety, but it's totally possible and completely worth it.

Let's talk more about the anxiety triggers that often come with going to college, as well as some other notable everyday life changes that may heavily impact people with anxiety issues — such as being a new parent, starting a new job, and dealing with family and relationship problems. I'll also go over some coping strategies you can use to manage your anxiety in specific situations.

## College

College is an exciting time for most people because it offers students the ability to live independently, make new friends, and explore new ideas — even in the midst of the hustle and bustle of final exams and graduation celebrations. These changes can oftentimes be challenging for college students, as well as high school students and parents who are thinking ahead. College students abruptly cut themselves off from their usual community of friends and family overnight, which can understandably be very stressful. At the same time, they have to learn how to manage a hefty workload, live with roommates, and establish an individual identity. It's no wonder that college students are so anxious!

If you're going to college soon, you might have some concerns about what's to come. This anxiety you're feeling is totally normal, but that doesn't mean it's easy to deal with. It might help to define and pinpoint your specific anxieties regarding college, so we'll delve into that next as well as go over some effective coping mechanisms you can use to make your college stress a little more manageable.

### What It Can Feel Like

Going to college can be scary — for students and parents alike. It's a whole new world, and as a student, you're being separated from your friends, family, and everything you know (usually for the first time). As a new college student, you might be concerned about living with a roommate and making new friends. You might wonder how you're going to manage your workload, because it's likely going to be heavier than it was in high school. College is also a time for self-discovery. This can be daunting for people with anxiety, but it can also be super exciting! You'll be independent from your parents and your hometown for the first time. It's the perfect opportunity to work on yourself and discover who you are as a person.

### What It Can Look Like

NEW COLLEGE STUDENTS will frequently experience homesickness, which is actually a form of separation anxiety. Chances are you've been homesick before. Maybe you missed your parents while at sleep-away camp when you were a kid, or perhaps you spent a week at your grandparents' house across the country and couldn't get over the feeling of wanting to go home. Homesickness is a common stress response for most new college students, especially those who are more introverted. The symptoms of homesickness in college students may include nausea, loss of appetite, trouble sleeping, shaking or trembling, muscle tension, fatigue, and struggling to pay attention and sit still while in class.

As an anxious college student, you may have trouble speaking up during lectures. Test-taking might be difficult for you, especially if you have anxiety in conjunction with ADHD (which is fairly common). You might struggle to turn in assignments on time, and, like Charles, you might keep to yourself and isolate in your dorm room rather than socialize with other students. You may begin to feel out of control, and like you just want to go home. These feelings are normal, but they can also be incredibly overwhelming. My advice is to stick with it. No matter how much you're struggling, things will get better with time. If you're really unhappy at your college, transferring schools is always an option as well.

## What Can You Do?

If you're a college student who's currently struggling with anxiety, there are a number of things you can do to help yourself feel better. The strategies listed below should help you quell your homesickness as well as be the best student you can be — both academically and socially. Keep in mind that it may take some time to find your niche and your people in college, but when you do, you'll forget that you were ever homesick in the first place.

### Keep a Normal Routine

As human beings, we thrive on routine. When you were in high school, you probably had a daily routine that worked quite well for you. Now that you're in college, you get to figure out a brand new daily routine for yourself. Make sure to keep your calendar updated with your class schedule. I used a whiteboard calendar, and hung it up next to my bed in my dorm room. I can't recommend this enough! Try not to overload yourself with schoolwork, as college isn't *just* about academics. Make time for friends, clubs, sports, or whatever else you're interested in.

## Watch Your Nutrition and Diet

Although living on pizza and instant ramen may be tempting, this type of diet isn't very good for your brain and body. Your school's dining hall may be relatively lackluster, but chances are, it at least has a salad bar. If you're on a meal plan — most college freshmen are — you shouldn't have any trouble getting your daily dose of proteins, carbs, fruits, and vegetables. I'm not saying you should deny yourself the occasional treat every once in a while. Just don't go overboard with it. Maintain a healthy diet, and your brain and body will be happy.

## Take Breaks

College students are prone to overworking themselves. This is especially true for students in STEM, although writing a 10-12 page literature paper is no walk in the park either. Remember to be realistic about your course load (especially as a freshman), and don't forget to take breaks every once in a while. For people with anxiety and ADHD, the Pomodoro technique can work wonders. Setting a Pomodoro timer will allow you to focus on your work for 25-minute increments while taking short breaks in between. It's a truly fantastic way to study. While taking breaks from studying, try going for a walk around campus or call up an old friend from home. You'll be able to return to your assignment feeling refreshed and ready to work.

### Find Resources on Campus

You'll have a difficult time finding a college campus that doesn't have a mental health resource center. If you've been struggling with anxiety, depression, or homesickness, don't be afraid to ask for help. You should be able to see a counselor on campus for relatively cheap as often as you need to. A good counselor will be able to help you organize your thoughts and take some of the emotional weight you've been feeling off your shoulders.

### Being a New Parent

This might feel like a bit of a jump, but hey — there are few things more stressful than being a new parent. Now that we've talked about some of the stressors that can trigger anxiety in college students, let's discuss the most anxiety-inducing parts of having a baby and being a parent for the first time. Like going to college, having a baby is a major milestone. Your whole life changes after you have a baby, which can send some new parents into a state of shock. New mothers in particular might experience postpartum depression (or postpartum anxiety, which isn't talked about quite as much).

Postpartum anxiety can be just as debilitating as postpartum depression. Most of the time, they go hand-in-hand. It's definitely not something that should be ignored or brushed aside. Postpartum anxiety symptoms generally take the form of intense worry, in contrast to postpartum depression, which can make new parents feel extremely depressed or even disinterested in their baby. The author of *The Hormone Cure*, Sara Gottfried, M.D., claims that you continuously feel nervous and tense while experiencing postpartum anxiety. "I think of postpartum anxiety as the loss of a normal sense of balance and calm, and postpartum depression as a loss of heart," she states. Let's discuss what postpartum anxiety can feel like below, as that should help you gain a deeper understanding of it.

### What It Can Feel Like

Those who are suffering from postpartum anxiety will typically go through bouts of insomnia due to their intense anxious feelings. Basically, they're plagued by the fear that their baby will stop breathing in their sleep, even if the baby is perfectly healthy. If you have postpartum anxiety, you might be afraid to leave your baby alone for a few minutes with an adult you trust — even your spouse. Sometimes, postpartum anxiety can ignite acute agoraphobia in new parents. You might be afraid to leave your house due to the fear of someone hurting you or your baby. You might spend a lot of time worrying about the worst-case scenarios — so much so that you won't be able to enjoy all of the wonderful parts of being a new parent.

### What It Can Look Like

If you've been diagnosed with postpartum anxiety, you may experience physical symptoms, such as nausea, loss of appetite, and shortness of breath. You might avoid certain people and activities, or have trouble relaxing and sitting still. Some postpartum anxiety sufferers will get into the habit of checking things over and over again (which is a symptom that is oftentimes related to OCD). Usually, this stems from the tendency to be overly cautious, even in situations that aren't dangerous. You're more likely to experience postpartum anxiety if you have a history of it in your family, or if your hormones are fluctuating a lot — which tends to happen to most mothers shortly after giving birth.

## What Can You Do?

IF YOU'RE HAVING a hard time with being a new parent, you're definitely not alone. Being a new parent is *hard* work, and it makes sense that you'd feel anxious (and exhausted) from time to time. If you're suffering from postpartum depression or postpartum anxiety, being a new parent can be even more challenging. Here are a few things you can do if you're struggling during those first few months of parenthood.

**Cuddle Your Baby**

Cuddling with your baby is a great way to bond with them. Spend enough time cuddling and holding your baby, and you might just find that this activity is beneficial for both of you. When you cuddle your baby, your brain releases oxytocin. This can significantly reduce your anxiety, as well as make your baby feel loved and safe. (Pro tip: Try smelling the top of your newborn's head when you're feeling particularly anxious. This smell is usually quite pleasant and can be incredibly comforting for new parents).

**Develop a Support System**

Raising a new baby is hard, but you don't have to do it alone. Hopefully, you have a supportive partner and family members who are willing to help out once in a while. Trust me — your mom wants nothing more than to love and spoil your little one. That's what grandmas are for! There are also plenty of online support groups for new parents who are struggling, so if you're a single parent and you don't live close to your parents, that might be something to look into.

### Take Care of Yourself

New parents have a tendency to forget about their own needs and focus solely on the needs of their baby. While taking care of your baby is important, you should also make sure that your own needs are being met. Try to maintain a healthy diet, and sleep as much as you can. It may be a little rough for those first few months, but it will get easier! Just keep trucking along.

## Family/Significant Other

There's a reason the holidays are such a stressful time for most people, and that reason is — unfortunately — family. Now, I love my family, but there's no denying that they can be a little much at times. Perhaps you feel the same way. Being around one's parents (and extended family in particular) can be anxiety-inducing for adults who have been living on their own for a long time. When you bring your significant other into the mix, it can make the situation all the more stressful. You might be concerned about how your family will treat your significant other, or you might worry that your partner won't like your family.

## What It Can Feel Like

People with anxiety are typically afraid of conflict, so it makes sense that reuniting with family members you've had conflicts with in the past would ignite some anxious feelings within you. Young adults who aren't following in their parents' footsteps (i.e. perhaps you became an artist instead of a doctor) might feel pressured by their parents to pursue a different career path. This can be frustrating, invalidating, and very, very anxiety-inducing — but remember: you're an adult and you get to be your own person.

It's also common for young adults with anxiety to dread the questions their parents are going to ask them or their significant other at the dinner table. Nobody wants to feel like they're being interviewed over Thanksgiving dinner, after all. Try to keep in mind that you don't have to answer any questions you don't want to answer. Your parents are only asking these questions because they love and care about you, but you're allowed to tell them if they're being too nosy!

## *What It Can Look Like*

PEOPLE WITH ANXIETY disorders might find themselves reverting back to child-like behavior when they're forced to spend more time than they're accustomed to spending with their parents and siblings. You might find yourself throwing tantrums or arguing with your sister, like you did when you were a teenager. While this can be an alarming experience, it's quite normal, and it stems from anxiety. This holiday season, try to be aware of your own behavior, and in the face of conflict, try to be the bigger person. This should help you to feel less anxious.

## *What Can You Do?*

There are a number of things you can do to quell your anxious feelings when you're spending time with family. One of the best things you can do is anticipate any potential triggers. If you know that your mom is going to start asking you questions about work, for example, you can decide ahead of time how you're going to respond to those questions. You should also try to keep comforting people (and pets!) close by. If your partner is your rock, then stick by them and confide in them when your family is making you feel anxious or depressed. Hugging your dog once in a while can't hurt, either!

Try to stay grounded in the present, and don't take anything that your parents or siblings say personally. It's also important that you speak up for yourself when a family member has hurt your feelings. Sometimes, our loved ones hurt us without even realizing it. Speaking up for yourself may be a great way to prevent a certain family member from sticking their foot in their mouth again. It's also a good idea to set some boundaries if your family members are particularly nosy. For example, your parents have got to keep in mind that you're an adult now, and they can't just barge into the bedroom that you and your partner are sharing while you're there.

## Work

Ah, yes... work. Is there any daily activity that's more stressful than work? Feeling concerned, anxious, uncomfortable, or tense about one's job or one's relationships with coworkers is often referred to as workplace anxiety. Anxiety at work is widespread; studies show that over 40% of Americans say they experience workplace stress on the daily. While a little bit of stress at work is normal, excessive workplace anxiety can have a detrimental impact on your mental health and physical well-being. This may cause issues in both your personal and professional lives if you don't know how to cope with it.

## What It Can Feel Like

Granted, when it comes to work, there are usually a lot of things to be stressed out about. Depending on the type of job you have, you might have to talk on the phone a lot or interact with customers who don't seem to understand basic human decency. I worked in food service throughout my twenties, so trust me — I get it. People with workplace anxiety will often worry about things like driving to work, making small talk with their colleagues, giving presentations, and speaking up in meetings. Some may stress out about finances if their job doesn't pay them enough. Most minimum-wage employees have to take a second job or a side gig to afford the cost of living these days, which only adds to their workplace anxiety.

## What It Can Look Like

Those who are struggling with workplace anxiety may fail to meet deadlines or take too long to complete tasks they would normally have no trouble completing. If you have anxiety at work, you might have a difficult time concentrating during meetings and interactions with customers. You may start taking more sick days to avoid going to work, or you may develop some somatic symptoms — such as headaches, dizziness, and an upset stomach. People with workplace anxiety tend to get burnt out more quickly than people who don't suffer from this type of anxiety. This burnt-out feeling can spill over into your personal life, and affect your non-work-related relationships.

### What Can You Do?

If you're currently suffering from workplace anxiety, you should know that you're not alone and that this feeling won't last forever. It's very important that you acknowledge your stressed-out feelings and talk to someone you trust about what you're going through. If you have a good manager, they can be a good support system for you, as can a friendly coworker. Remember to take breaks while at work. When I was working a particularly stressful job, I always found it helpful to put on my headphones and take a quick walk around the block. It's also important to know your limits and work within those limits. The number one thing that causes burnout and workplace anxiety is working too much, so just keep that in mind.

## Segue

Keeping track of the things that trigger your anxiety on a daily basis can be incredibly helpful, as can utilizing the various coping mechanisms outlined in this chapter. In the next section, I'll dive into anxiety triggers that typically stem from trauma — such as the trauma we maintain from childhood or past relationships.

## 5

## TRIGGER 3: WHEN THINGS GET PERSONAL...

*"In order to move on, you must understand why you felt what you did and why you no longer need to feel it."*

— MITCH ALBOM

For many people, their anxiety stems from past trauma, mostly (but not always) from childhood. The events that happen to you during your childhood are essentially the building blocks that make up the foundation for your adulthood. These events don't define who you are, but they *happened* — and the sooner you're able to accept that they happened, the sooner you'll be able to let go and live your adult life without these unfortunate events looming over you. This is easier said than done, but it isn't something you have to conquer on your own.

The fact of the matter is, if your childhood trauma is the main thing that's been triggering your adult anxiety (as is the case for many people), then something must be done about it. Thankfully, there are plenty of coping strategies you can use to help yourself in situations where your anxiety is getting triggered due to past traumatic experiences. One of the most effective ways to process childhood trauma is to participate in Cognitive Behavioral Therapy. CBT is one of the best PTSD treatments out there, and considering the fact that anxiety tends to go hand-in-hand with PTSD, it's no surprise that CBT has been proven to help anxiety patients with trauma-related anxiety triggers.

A friend of mine (who I'll call "Maddy") gave me permission to share the following story with you. When Maddy was a little girl, she had a difficult home life. You would never guess that this was the case because she went to school with a smile every day and was generally very curious about the world. Little did her teachers and classmates know, her parents got into screaming matches almost every night. Her father was an alcoholic, and he would oftentimes lash out at Maddy when she tried to stand up for her mother.

Her mother eventually became emotionally unavailable and distant towards her, despite Maddy's efforts to help her. Of course, Maddy should never have been put in that position in the first place. She was only nine years old. She started developing symptoms of anxiety and PTSD, like insomnia and nightmares. She had trouble eating and began to have panic attacks at school on a regular basis. Her dad, at this point, was too far gone, and her mom dismissed her symptoms as being overly sensitive.

When Maddy turned ten, her dad left in the middle of the night and never came back. This meant that Maddy's mom had to raise her on her own. Although both of them felt some relief after Maddy's dad left, Maddy's mom was struggling to make ends meet. She started taking double shifts at work, which meant Maddy was left alone for hours at a time. She began to feel lonely and sad, and with no one to share her worries with, she eventually started self-harming.

After a few months, Maddy's mother noticed the scars covering her daughter's arms. She decided to take Maddy to a therapist, who — after years of Cognitive Behavioral Therapy — helped Maddy understand the ways in which her traumatic past impacted her mental health. By the time she was sixteen, Maddy learned how to utilize certain coping strategies, such as mindfulness and journaling. She also learned how to express her thoughts and emotions, which allowed her to begin to heal from the trauma she'd experienced.

As Maddy grew older, she gained confidence and independence. She excelled in school, made new friends, and even landed her dream job as a wildlife conservationist. She learned how to recognize and cope with her anxiety triggers — which included things like men yelling and children crying. She also learned how to set necessary boundaries with those who had hurt her in the past, which allowed her to prioritize her mental health.

Despite going through trauma during her childhood, Maddy was eventually able to overcome her anxiety and thrive as an adult. It wasn't easy, and it admittedly took some time, but going through this healing process was absolutely crucial to her adult happiness. Her past trauma had been preventing her from living her life to the fullest, and she didn't want that to be the case forever.

If you're struggling with anxiety triggers brought on by past trauma, you're definitely not alone. In this chapter, we'll discuss both childhood trauma and relationship trauma as significantly impactful anxiety triggers. Let's take a closer look at what these past traumas can look and feel like, as well as go over some coping strategies you can use to quell your anxious feelings after you've been triggered.

This may be a difficult chapter for some people, so feel free to skip it now and come back to it when you're ready. Being uncomfortable is a big part of the healing process, but you shouldn't have to be uncomfortable until you're ready to be uncomfortable. Just keep that in mind. Without further ado, let's get into it, shall we?

## (Childhood) Trauma

Experiencing childhood trauma can certainly increase one's risk of developing anxiety disorders, like PTSD, OCD, and Social Anxiety Disorder. As I mentioned previously, the best way to address your feelings of anxiety — once you've been triggered — is to confront your trauma directly. It's also important to remember that anxiety is a common condition, so you're not going through this alone. As we've already learned, anxiety can manifest in several different forms, such as persistent and intense worry about everyday situations. Those who have been through childhood trauma are statistically more likely to experience these types of symptoms, which can sometimes lead to the development of an anxiety disorder.

Childhood trauma is a well-known phenomenon, and it's something that can stay with us throughout our lives. Oftentimes, childhood trauma can cause anxiety that we may not even realize is rooted in past experiences. Even when we do recognize the source of our trauma, it can be difficult to deal with and move past for most people. The reason childhood trauma tends to linger is that we often suppress it, which tends to manifest as PTSD over time. It's a natural tendency to avoid painful situations, but burying your problems is ultimately more harmful than it is helpful.

Your childhood experiences, both good and bad, have shaped who you are today. The people you were surrounded by as a kid (i.e. family, friends, teachers, and strangers) have all impacted you in different ways. Unfortunately, as children, it's not uncommon for us to be hurt by the adults in our lives — which can lead to a general feeling of distrust in those who suffer from anxiety and PTSD. It's important to recognize that exploring issues like anxiety will usually involve looking back at your past experiences. You've got to acknowledge and address your past traumas in order to effectively move forward and heal.

## *What It Can Feel Like*

CHILDHOOD TRAUMA-BASED anxiety is a complicated problem, and it's not something that's easy for most people to deal with. The thing about childhood trauma-based anxiety is, you never really know how it's going to manifest. Some people might feel like they're worrying all the time, even if things aren't actually that bad. Others might be on edge and unable to relax, or feel restless a lot of the time. Emotions can be intense and unpredictable, making it hard to feel like you're in control. It's also pretty common to feel like you're always on guard, and those with PTSD might have repetitive dreams or memories that are especially distressing.

Unfortunately, some people turn to drugs or alcohol to help deal with all of these feelings, which can make matters worse. On top of that, it can be really hard to concentrate, or to stop thinking about all the worst possible outcomes of any given situation. Making decisions is particularly difficult when you're dealing with this kind of anxiety, because it feels like there's always something to worry about. Letting go of your worries can be almost impossible, and some may feel like they'll be stuck with their worries for the rest of their life. This, in a nutshell, is what childhood trauma-based anxiety can feel like.

## *What It Can Look Like*

Again, there's no telling how childhood trauma-based anxiety is going to manifest. It typically depends on the person and the experiences they've been through. That said, this type of anxiety might make it particularly difficult for you to fall asleep, which means you might be exhausted during the day a lot of the time. You might notice concerning changes in your behavior, or feel like your thoughts are out of control.

It's also not uncommon for people with childhood trauma-based anxiety to experience physical symptoms — such as muscle tension, twitchiness, and extreme sensitivity to one's environment. Everyday situations might feel like too much to handle, and you may feel especially jumpy in situations that are somewhat triggering (even if that particular situation is not, in and of itself, dangerous). Due to constantly being on edge, you may occasionally feel sick to your stomach. You might feel like you're being watched or overanalyze other people's reactions to certain situations. These feelings and symptoms can be difficult to deal with, and they can ultimately take a significant toll on your relationships with others.

## What Can You Do?

IF YOU'RE STRUGGLING with anxiety that stems from childhood trauma, there are thankfully a number of things you can do to help yourself feel better. My friend, Maddy, probably would have had a much harder time dealing with her anxiety had she not gotten serious about doing what was necessary to heal after going through trauma. Let's go over some of the most effective coping strategies that I came across in my research below.

### Cognitive Behavioral Therapy (CBT)

In trauma-based Cognitive Behavioral Therapy, a therapist helps you recognize your negative thought patterns that are related to the traumatic events you've experienced and challenges them. They help you understand that these thoughts are unproductive and that they're negatively impacting your well-being and personal relationships. In CBT, you work with the therapist on replacing your harmful thought patterns with more positive and realistic ones. This process takes time and patience, but it can eventually help you heal and move forward, so it's definitely worth it.

### Prolonged Exposure (PE) Therapy

This type of therapy can be very helpful for people with severe PTSD. The idea behind PE is to gradually expose the anxiety patient to their traumatic memories and experiences in a safe and controlled environment. Over time, this exposure can help to reduce the fear and anxiety the person associates with these memories, which will eventually allow them to process and come to terms with what happened during their childhood. PE is often used in conjunction with other forms of therapy, such as CBT, to provide a more effective approach to treating childhood trauma-based anxiety.

### Face Your Feelings

When it comes to coping with childhood trauma-based anxiety, facing your feelings head-on can be daunting. However, it's a necessary step toward healing. It can be tempting to push painful emotions aside or bury them deep down, but the truth is that these feelings will only continue to fester if you bottle them up. By acknowledging and allowing yourself to feel your emotions, you can begin to process and work through them in a healthy way. Although it may be difficult at first, it will ultimately be well worth it.

### Prioritize Self-Care

Needless to say, trauma can take a huge toll on both your mental and physical health. For this reason, it's important that you make time for self-care activities as they can help you feel more grounded. Self-care can include meditation, journaling, physical exercise, spending time in nature, or simply taking a few minutes to breathe and check in with yourself. It's also important to note that a big part of self-care is setting boundaries and learning to say no to things you don't want to do.

### Medication

Medication isn't always necessary, but it can be exceptionally helpful for some people who are struggling with extreme trauma-based anxiety. Talk with your therapist or healthcare provider about going on anti-anxiety or antidepressant medication if you feel like it might benefit you. Although there's some stigma surrounding using medication to treat mental health disorders, it's exceedingly common and is nothing to be ashamed of. Medication is typically used in tandem with CBT and Prolonged Exposure Therapy. Personally, I would only use this tactic as a last resort once you put the work in with other non-medicated therapies.

## Past Romantic Relationships

Now that we've discussed the ins and outs of childhood trauma-based anxiety, let's move on to a different type of anxiety trigger — trauma that stems from past romantic relationships. Have you ever felt doubts, insecurities, and a constant need for reassurance in a relationship, even when everything seems perfect? This is what's known as relationship anxiety. Relationship anxiety is a surprisingly common experience, and it can often stem from early childhood trauma. It usually indicates an insecure attachment style and severe abandonment or trust issues in people who suffer from this type of anxiety, however, that's not always the case.

For a person with relationship anxiety, questions like "Do they really like me?" and "How long until this falls apart?" can plague their thoughts, even if they've already exchanged "I love yous" with their partner. While it's normal to have some worries about a relationship, extreme anxiety can significantly impact its growth or even prevent a relationship from starting altogether. Let's take a closer look at how relationship anxiety can manifest, as well as what you can do to more effectively cope with your trauma from past relationships.

## What It Can Feel Like

FOR THOSE WHO suffer from relationship anxiety, it can feel all-consuming. This type of anxiety tends to take a major toll on your emotional well-being as well as your romantic relationships. It's like having a never-ending barrage of questions bombarding your mind — making you constantly question yourself, your partner, and the relationship as a whole. You might find yourself wondering whether or not you truly matter to your partner, or worry about the possibility of a breakup. You may frequently ask your partner for reassurance or validation, which can put a strain on your relationship.

Relationship anxiety may also lead you to doubt the long-term compatibility of your relationship, which could leave you feeling uneasy and uncertain about your future with your partner. These feelings can make it difficult for people with this type of anxiety to truly enjoy their romantic relationships, which is a saddening issue. Love is one of the best experiences in the world, and it's not fair that your anxiety is preventing you from fully experiencing all of the beauty that comes with it.

### Retrospective Jealousy

Have you ever felt uncomfortable or insecure when thinking about a romantic partner's past relationships or experiences? It's normal to feel a bit insecure about these kinds of things, but if it gets to the point of obsession, you might want to consider talking to a therapist about whether or not you could have relationship anxiety. This type of jealousy can be particularly difficult for anxious people to deal with because it's based on events that have already happened and cannot be changed.

That said, it's important to remember that your past relationships and experiences are a part of who you are. You might not be happy about some of your partner's past relationship choices, but at least they've been honest with you about those choices. The best thing you can do for yourself is focus on the present and the future of your relationship with this person, rather than dwell on the past. Communication and trust are key when it comes to overcoming retrospective jealousy and building a strong, healthy relationship.

### What It Can Look Like

Relationship anxiety affects everyone differently. However, some symptoms you can typically expect to come across include feeling unmotivated, tired, and emotionally drained. To make matters worse, these symptoms can also cause physical discomfort, like upset stomachs and headaches. People with relationship anxiety have a tendency to accidentally mess things up by starting arguments with their partner or by distancing themselves even though they're really upset. This could manifest in different ways, like hanging out with a toxic ex or overanalyzing their partner's words or actions.

People with relationship anxiety usually need a lot of reassurance from their partner. They might always want to be around their partner and be somewhat clingy, which could cause them to act a bit controlling at times. Some people with relationship anxiety might give their partner the silent treatment for the sake of avoiding conflict — or, they might do things to please their partner, even if it means giving up what they want.

There are plenty of reasons why someone might develop relationship anxiety. Perhaps they had a partner who cheated on them in the past, or maybe their first love broke up with them out of the blue. Other factors, such as low self-esteem, an insecure attachment style, or a tendency to doubt their partner's feelings can also contribute to relationship anxiety.

*What Can You Do?*

THANKFULLY, if you're suffering from relationship anxiety, there are certain actions you can take to help remedy the issue. One option that experts recommend for treating and managing relationship anxiety is couples therapy, which may include attending psychoeducational sessions with your partner. Let's go over some of the most effective coping strategies when it comes to overcoming relationship anxiety below.

**Maintain Your Identity**

As you and your partner get closer, you may begin to notice that some aspects of your identity or independence have started to shift in order to make space for the relationship. This is a common occurrence as couples become more intertwined. While certain adjustments, like adjusting to your partner's sleep schedule, may not affect your sense of self, others might have a more significant impact. It's important that you maintain a sense of self in every relationship you enter into. You shouldn't change yourself solely to please your partner, as this won't benefit either of you in the long run. It's very important that you communicate with your partner and find ways to compromise and grow together while still maintaining both of your individual identities.

**Confront Your Anxiety**

Charles and Maddy got where they are today because they learned how to confront their anxiety head-on. If you're having trouble confronting your relationship anxiety, a therapist should be able to help you do so. They should also be able to help you get used to normalizing feelings of jealousy. It's crucial to recognize that while these feelings are valid, they're not always logical.

**Practice Good Communication**

If you're struggling with anxiety in your relationship, it's absolutely essential that you have honest and open conversations with your partner about your worries and expectations for the future. Share any doubts you may have with them, and work through any challenges together. This will ultimately be much better than inventing worst-case scenarios in your head and getting angry with your partner for no reason they'll be able to understand.

**Cognitive Behavioral Conjoint Therapy**

Cognitive Behavioral Conjoint Therapy (CBCT) is a type of therapy that can help couples work through relationship anxiety. This type of therapy focuses specifically on identifying and changing negative thought patterns and behaviors that can cause anxiety and stress in a relationship. CBCT can help couples learn how to communicate more effectively with one another, as well as develop better problem-solving skills. With the guidance of a trained therapist, you and your partner will be able to learn how to relate to each other in new ways. This should eventually help you develop a healthier, more satisfying relationship.

**Enjoy the Present**

When it comes to being in a romantic relationship, there's nothing better than living in the moment. Focusing on the present moment can be an especially effective way to cope with relationship anxiety — especially for those with anxiety disorders. By enjoying the present, you'll be able to redirect your attention away from your worries and instead focus on living your best life with your partner. If you're having trouble enjoying the present, try doing fun activities with your partner — such as going for walks or cooking together. You should also put effort into being mindful of your thoughts and behaviors, as this will help you to become more attuned to your own emotions as well as those of your partner.

**Segue**

It can be especially difficult to face the anxiety triggers that stem from particularly personal issues — such as childhood trauma or problems you've had to deal with in past romantic relationships. However, confronting these triggers is a necessary part of healing and overcoming your anxiety in the long run. If you're struggling, consider meeting with a Cognitive Behavioral Therapist. Prioritize self-care and do your best to enjoy the present moment. In the next section, I'll dive a little deeper into social anxiety and the actions you can take to more effectively cope with it.

# 6

# TRIGGER 4: WHEN GET-TOGETHERS MAKE YOU FALL APART...

*"You wouldn't worry so much about what others think of you if you realized how seldom they do."*

— ELEANOR ROOSEVELT

Social anxiety can be a particularly difficult beast to tame. It's surprising how common social anxiety is, however, there's some confusion surrounding it because it's often misread as introversion — which may slightly overlap with social anxiety, but it's ultimately not the same thing. Unlike run-of-the-mill introversion, social anxiety can be an overwhelming and paralyzing experience for a lot of people. The mere thought of being in a crowded room or making small talk with a group of strangers can trigger a flood of uncomfortable emotions and physical sensations for people who struggle with social anxiety.

Some people with this type of anxiety may experience symptoms like sweaty palms, increased heart rate, racing thoughts, and an upset stomach. It can make it very difficult to be around other people, and not just in the context of parties and get-togethers. Even just going to the grocery store can feel like an insurmountable task for someone with social anxiety.

Social anxiety is oftentimes deeply rooted in the fear of being judged or rejected — which may or may not stem from past trauma for some people. This fear can lead those with social anxiety to avoid social situations altogether. Take Charles, for instance. When he was in his mid-twenties, he seldom went to get-togethers with his friends because his social anxiety was so bad. He always seemed to have an excuse for why he couldn't make it to this and that get-together. "I'm too tired," he'd tell us. "I have to be up early tomorrow," etc., etc.

Some people in our friend group began to wonder if Charles didn't like hanging out with them. They became concerned and eventually annoyed that he never seemed to want to spend any time with them. Little did they know, Charles would have loved to get together with us to see a movie or go out for drinks. It was just that he was under the control of his social anxiety. Charles was aware that some people in our friend group were irritated with him, too, which only made his anxiety worse. (There's a lesson in here about being patient with your friends who struggle with social anxiety. They *want* to spend time with you, but their anxiety makes it very difficult for them to do so.)

Eventually, Charles started talking to a therapist about his social anxiety. She taught him about some techniques and strategies he could use to more effectively cope with being anxious in public. He learned how to talk back to his negative thoughts, and after a while, was able to reframe them completely. He realized that catastrophizing and ruminating about being judged by his friends was ultimately unhelpful and unproductive. It took some time for him to reframe his anxious thoughts into more productive ones, but it was time well-spent. I think he'd definitely agree that it was worth it.

Although Charles is doing much better now, he still has to work extra hard to be fully present in social situations. He practices mindful breathing before and during get-togethers in order to avoid letting his social anxiety get the best of him. Some days are more difficult than others, but he's learned to be patient with himself — and his friends who previously misunderstood what he was going through have learned to be patient with him as well.

It's important to keep in mind that overcoming social anxiety is a marathon, not a sprint. Like Charles, you might experience some especially hard days here and there, even after you've put the work in to properly address your social anxiety. When the going gets tough, remember to breathe and have compassion for yourself. Coping with social anxiety isn't easy, but it's definitely possible if you're willing to put the time and effort in.

In this chapter, we'll do a deep dive into social anxiety. Social anxiety is oftentimes misunderstood. There's a lot of misinformation out there — which can make things worse for socially anxious people who can't stop themselves from Googling the symptoms. I want to use this opportunity to clear some things up. What *is* social anxiety, exactly? What are the most common root causes of this unique type of anxiety, and what sort of daily activities tend to trigger it? We'll go over all of this and more in this chapter, so if you've been struggling with social anxiety, don't fret! Taking back your life is totally possible, just as long as you have the right information and tools on hand.

## What is Social Anxiety?

Social anxiety disorder is an extremely common form of anxiety that many people struggle with. In other words, if you're currently battling social anxiety, you're not alone. This debilitating condition can make it difficult to engage in social situations, even with friends and other loved ones, especially if the socially anxious person feels judged or scrutinized in any way. A person with social anxiety may have difficulty speaking in public, going on dates, attending job interviews, or even just talking to a cashier at the grocery store. Simple tasks like eating or drinking in front of other people can trigger social anxiety for some, as they may fear being humiliated or rejected based on the way others perceive them.

The fear that comes with social anxiety disorder is often so intense that it feels impossible to control. For some people, it can prevent them from going to work or school. Others may be able to push through, but they'll still experience a lot of fear and anxiety, and be totally exhausted when they get home. It's not uncommon for people with this type of anxiety to worry about upcoming social situations for weeks in advance, and some may end up avoiding certain places or events altogether.

While some people with social anxiety disorder

only experience anxious thoughts or symptoms during performances (i.e. giving speeches, playing music on stage, competing in sports, etc.), others may experience anxiety that gets triggered by any type of social interaction. Social anxiety disorder typically develops in late childhood and can oftentimes be misread as extreme shyness or introversion. Social anxiety disorder is also more common in women than in men, especially among teenagers and young adults. If left untreated, social anxiety disorder may last for several years (or even a lifetime for some).

## Common Root Causes of Social Anxiety

Social anxiety is more complicated than most people realize. It can be caused by a lot of different factors, or, a combination of factors — including genetics, environmental issues, cognitive biases, and cultural influences. Genetics definitely plays a significant role in the development of social anxiety for some. Experts have identified the SLCGA4 (serotonin transporter) gene as a potential contributor to social anxiety. Those who have socially anxious parents are also more likely to develop social anxiety disorder. It basically has a lot to do with the effects of nature and nurture. Let's go over some of the most common root causes of social anxiety below.

## *Parental Shortcomings*

You're unfortunately more likely to develop social anxiety if you grew up with parents who were overcontrolling, quick to criticize, reluctant to show affection, or overly concerned about the opinions of other people. Kids who grow up in these types of environments are at risk of developing an insecure attachment style, which can end up manifesting as social anxiety later in life. Older siblings who are burdened with the task of caring for their younger brothers and sisters when their parents aren't around are also at risk of developing social anxiety.

## *Social Trauma*

When Charles was in high school, he got bullied relentlessly by this group of guys that just could not seem to leave him alone. This undoubtedly contributed to the social anxiety he experienced as an adult. Traumatic social experiences — like being bullied or teased by your peers — can definitely cause a person to develop social anxiety disorder. Witnessing other people's traumatic social experiences can also lead to the development of this disorder, especially if you've been through the trauma you're witnessing yourself.

## Lack of Social Skills

While some people are natural social butterflies, others just aren't — which is perfectly okay. Factors like introversion, ADHD, and Autism can sometimes play a role in a person's lack of social skills, but this isn't always the case. Sometimes, being social is just difficult. As an introvert, this is something I've come to understand quite well.

If you struggle to communicate effectively with others or have difficulties forming relationships in general, it may be because you have social anxiety. These struggles can also lead to the development of social anxiety. If you're not really sure what's going on with your brain, it might be a good idea to meet with a therapist. They should be able to provide you with some much-needed clarity, which will in turn help to quell your anxiety.

## Cognitive Biases

Cognitive biases can have a profound impact on one's mental health. These biases refer to the unfavorable ways of thinking that can potentially lead some people to perceive themselves in a negative light. In short, cognitive biases are thought patterns that can distort a person's perceptions of reality. This means that someone with deeply-rooted cognitive biases might misinterpret certain social situations and interactions.

For example, a common cognitive bias that someone with social anxiety might experience is "catastrophic thinking." A person with the "catastrophic thinking" cognitive bias is basically hardwired to believe that the worst possible outcome will happen if they go to a certain social event, which is why people with social anxiety tend to avoid get-togethers with friends or coworkers. The negative thoughts and emotions that stem from this social avoidance can sometimes get so overwhelming that the socially anxious person might end up developing depression in conjunction with social anxiety.

## Cultural Differences

Social anxiety is a universal phenomenon. Naturally, it can affect people across different cultures. However, the ways in which social anxiety manifests and the specific things that trigger it can vary depending on how a specific culture does things. For example, in individualistic cultures, such as the United States, socially anxious people may be triggered by the fear of not being perceived as independent or self-sufficient. In collectivistic cultures, such as Japan, however, people with social anxiety might get triggered by the fear of not fitting in with a certain group or failing to meet group expectations.

Cultural differences in communication styles and social norms can also contribute to the development of social anxiety in some people. In many cultures, direct communication and assertiveness tend to be valued, while in others, indirect communication and avoidance of confrontation are preferred. This can oftentimes lead to confusion and anxiety for those who are not familiar with a certain culture's particular communication style.

## Symptoms of Social Anxiety

We've all been in situations where we feel nervous or uneasy around others. Maybe you've felt shy or anxious when meeting someone new or before giving a big presentation at work. Walking into a room full of strangers or speaking in public isn't everyone's cup of tea, but most people are able to manage it.

However, if you have social anxiety disorder, these situations can be too overwhelming to handle. You might start to avoid all social interactions because things that most people consider normal, like engaging in small talk or making eye contact while having a conversation, make you feel extremely uncomfortable. This can affect all aspects of your life, not just your social life — which could potentially lead to a mental breakdown if you ignore or brush aside your social anxiety for too long. Let's go over some of the symptoms that are most commonly associated with social anxiety below so that you can gain a deeper understanding of what you've been experiencing.

### Emotional and Behavioral Symptoms

Social anxiety can cause a lot of emotional and behavioral symptoms, which can end up making simple tasks — like grocery shopping, or taking your dog for a walk in a busy park — exceptionally difficult. One of the most common symptoms people with social anxiety experience is the fear of being perceived in a negative light by other people. This fear can make a social situation, like a get-together, particularly stressful for a socially anxious person, as he may spend the entire evening panicking about whether or not he might embarrass himself.

As I've already briefly mentioned, people with social anxiety tend to avoid social events. They may isolate themselves in order to avoid potential embarrassment, and they're likely to feel uncomfortable when they're in a position where they're the center of attention (such as a surprise birthday party, for example). People with social anxiety may worry a lot before, during, and after social events. Some may even analyze their social performance after the fact, and beat themselves up if they feel like they didn't do well enough.

People with social anxiety also tend to have trouble making eye contact or speaking up when in social situations. These symptoms can make it exceptionally difficult for people with this affliction to form and maintain meaningful relationships with others, do well at work or in school, and enjoy all that life has to offer.

### Physical Symptoms

Unsurprisingly, social anxiety doesn't come without some unpleasant physical symptoms as well. It can essentially make you feel like your body is betraying you. You might turn red as a tomato while talking to someone you have a crush on, or your hands might tremble uncontrollably while you're giving a presentation at work. In some situations, you may feel like you're going to puke your guts out. You might struggle to catch your breath at times, which can cause lightheadedness and even fainting in rare cases.

You might find yourself crying a lot in situations where you feel overwhelmed, or you might feel like your mind has gone blank when someone asks you a question — even if you're an expert on whatever it is they're asking about. All of these physical symptoms can make social situations feel unbearable, but it's important to remember that you're not alone. If you've been experiencing any of the symptoms listed above, don't hesitate to reach out for help. There are plenty of ways to manage your social anxiety symptoms, and eventually overcome them — which we'll dive into next.

## Social Anxiety Triggers

When it comes to managing social anxiety, identifying your triggers is the first necessary step you'll need to take. This may be easier said than done, especially considering the fact that a lot of different things can trigger social anxiety. It usually depends on the person and their past experiences, however, there are some common social anxiety triggers that you'll want to keep in mind.

### *Meeting New People*

Walking into a room full of strangers is daunting for most people, but for those with social anxiety disorder, it can feel like an insurmountable task. The fear of being judged negatively by others can be incredibly overwhelming for some. If you have this particular fear, it may cause you to worry about potentially embarrassing or humiliating yourself in public. Even simple actions like maintaining eye contact or making small talk with a coworker can feel like scaling a mountain for those who suffer from social anxiety.

## Dating

Dating can be a nerve-wracking experience, and for those with social anxiety disorder, it can feel like an impossible challenge. The thought of putting oneself out there, texting, making phone calls, and going on dates can be overwhelming — which may trigger symptoms of anxiety in some (or frankly most) people. It's important to keep in mind that for someone with social anxiety disorder, the fear of judgment and rejection can be paralyzing. They may worry that they won't measure up to their date's expectations, or that they'll embarrass themselves somehow. This fear can lead to certain behaviors that may confuse a socially anxious person's partner, such as canceling plans, declining date invitations, or even ghosting. Needless to say, this can inhibit a socially anxious person's ability to form romantic relationships.

## Asking For Help From Customer Service Personnel

This is a big one. Despite the fact that customer service people are literally there to help you, you might find that you're unable to ask for the help you need if you suffer from social anxiety. I've been through a fair amount of social anxiety myself, and the fear of "annoying" a service worker with questions that may seem "stupid" or "obvious" is a very real thing. When I was in my early twenties, I didn't want to be perceived as annoying, so I avoided asking service workers for help. Similarly, I refused to send back incorrect meals or return things I'd purchased from the store that I was unsatisfied with — just because I didn't want to irritate the service workers. Remember, helping you is literally their job, so don't be afraid to ask for help when you need it.

### Eating, Drinking, Reading, Writing, Typing... and Just Generally Existing in Front of Others

When you have social anxiety, everything you do can feel embarrassing — especially if there are other people around to perceive you, you know... living your life. It's important to keep in mind that everyone else is just trying to live their lives, too. In general, other people are too concerned with their own issues to even notice what you're doing in public. Nobody is going to judge you for reading, writing, eating, drinking, etc. in public because they're too busy worrying about being judged by other people for doing these exact things. Take a deep breath, and exist. Nobody is going to care that much about what you're doing in a public setting (as long as you're not streaking or running around yelling "purple hippo!" in people's faces). Just live your life! It's all going to be okay.

### Being Teased

People with social anxiety tend to take being teased very personally. More often than not, those who suffer from social anxiety are Highly Sensitive People (HSP) which means they're extremely empathetic and may feel emotions on a deeper level than the average person. If you have social anxiety, you might not always pick up on the fact that a friend is teasing you. It's very easy for people with social anxiety to fall into a pit of negative thoughts, and teasing can sometimes trigger this.

### Speaking on the Phone

There's a reason so many young people prefer texting over phone calls. Phone calls are anxiety-inducing! Older folks might prefer phone calls over texting because that's what they're used to, but the opposite is true for younger people. It can be especially difficult for people with social anxiety to talk on the phone with strangers or people they haven't talked to in a long time.

This can make jobs where you have to cold call clients or deal with unsatisfied customers over the phone really difficult for those who have social anxiety.

## Ways to Cope With Social Anxiety

It's easy to feel helpless when it comes to the overwhelming symptoms of social anxiety disorder, but there are actually plenty of things you can do to help manage it. The first step is to change your mindset. People with social anxiety often have negative thoughts and beliefs that only further fuel their fears and anxieties. These negative thoughts may include:

> "I'm sure I'll look like an idiot."
> "My voice will start shaking, and everyone will see how nervous I am."
> "People will think I'm so boring and stupid."
> "I won't know what to say, and everyone will see how awkward I am."

Challenging these thoughts is an effective way to begin tackling your social anxiety symptoms. It's important to remind yourself that these are just thoughts, and your thoughts are not necessarily reality. Try to find evidence to refute your negative beliefs, and focus on the positive aspects when faced with a social situation.

With time and practice, you can eventually change the way you think and overcome your social anxiety. Let's take a look at some coping strategies you can use to combat your social anxiety when you feel like you've been triggered.

### Control Your Breathing

When anxiety takes hold, a cascade of physiological changes occurs in your body. Rapid breathing (or hyperventilation), for example, can disrupt the balance of oxygen and carbon dioxide within your system. This can end up triggering even more unpleasant physical symptoms — such as dizziness, a racing heart rate, and shortness of breath. The good news is, taking control of your breathing can help you regain balance in your body and alleviate some of these nasty physical symptoms. When practicing breath control, remember to sit comfortably and inhale slowly. Hold your breath for two seconds, exhale slowly, and repeat. Eventually, you'll notice yourself starting to feel better.

## Face Your Fears

FACING your fears is key when it comes to coping with social anxiety, however, you don't want to bite off more than you can chew. Rather than attempting to face your biggest fear right away, try starting with something small. Perhaps you can strike up a conversation with a stranger at the grocery store, or invite your neighbor in for a cup of coffee sometime. If you have trouble with social interactions, training yourself to be more social can work wonders. It can alleviate your social fears and anxiety, which means you'll be able to lead a more fulfilling social life.

## Try Progressive Muscle Relaxation

Progressive muscle relaxation is a technique that teaches you how to unwind your muscles when you're feeling stressed out. All you have to do is follow two simple steps. First, you tense up certain muscle groups like your neck and shoulders in the order that makes the most sense to you. Then, you let go of all that tightness and feel how your muscles loosen up. This exercise can be a lifesaver when you're feeling super anxious, as it can help you lower the tension levels in your body. It can even help with things like stom-achaches, headaches, and insomnia — which is definitely a plus! Give it a try and see how it works for you.

## Take the Focus Off of Yourself

Social anxiety tends to stem from insecurity and self-consciousness in social situations, typically due to past events and experiences. When you're in a nerve-wracking social situation, you should try to focus your attention on the people around you (but not on what they're thinking about you). Your anxiety isn't as visible as you think, so it's really not worth worrying about. Do your best to focus on and enjoy the present moment, or, in other words, don't let your anxiety hold you back from having a good time with your loved ones.

## Challenge and Talk Back to Negative Thoughts

If you want to tackle your social anxiety at its core, you've got to challenge the negative thoughts that fuel it. This involves figuring out which thoughts trigger your anxiety or make you feel awkward in social situations, and questioning them. You also need to challenge the underlying beliefs (cognitive biases) that back up your negative thoughts. By doing so, you can start to reframe your thinking and talk back to your negative thoughts when they're getting you down.

### Attend Cognitive Behavioral Therapy

Social anxiety disorder (and other anxiety disorders) can frequently be treated with cognitive behavioral therapy — which we've already touched on quite a bit. Studies show that cognitive behavioral therapy is a super effective way to treat social anxiety disorder, so it's definitely worth a shot. Cognitive behavioral therapy uses a combination of techniques, which essentially means you'll be tackling your social anxiety from all angles when you engage in CBT.

### Medication

Certain medications, such as Benzodiazepines, antidepressants, and beta blockers, can be very helpful for those who are struggling with social anxiety. If you feel like medication might be helpful for you, talk to your therapist or doctor about your options. It's not necessarily a good idea to become too reliant on anti-anxiety medications, but they can be incredibly beneficial for those who need to get back on their feet after going through a breakdown.

## Segue

Social anxiety is a unique beast, but if you have the right tools and know-how, you shouldn't have any trouble slaying it. Some common social anxiety triggers include meeting new people, asking for help, talking on the phone, and being teased. It's very important that you don't *avoid* these triggers, but *face* them instead. Confronting your social anxiety head-on is ultimately going to be what helps you overcome it in the long run. In the next chapter, I'll talk more about anxiety management techniques. This will include a couple of mindfulness exercises that you can try out on your own.

# 7

# ANXIETY MANAGEMENT TECHNIQUES

*"You may not control all the events that happen to you, but you can decide not to be reduced by them."*

— MAYA ANGELOU

Anxiety simply isn't talked about enough due to the stigma that surrounds it. This definitely needs to change. How are people supposed to know how to manage their anxiety if no one ever broaches the subject? There are, thankfully, quite a lot of relaxation and mindfulness techniques out there that have gained popularity among people who struggle with anxiety — especially today. The fact that mindfulness has become so deeply integrated into a lot of people's daily routines, work lives, and sleep regimens is a sign that society is headed in the right direction in terms of taking anxiety disorders more seriously.

Charles is a pretty good example of someone who was afraid to get help for his anxiety issues because of the stigma he'd experienced and read about online. The thing was, Charles knew he needed help, but he'd heard way too many stories about people with anxiety losing their jobs or being labeled as "weak" or "crazy" by their friends and family members. He didn't want to be judged or ostracized by the people he loved, so he kept his feelings bottled up — which, of course, only made things worse.

His anxiety started to affect his job, as well as his relationship with his girlfriend. He began to isolate himself from his friends and refused to attend social gatherings because the thought alone made him sick with worry. After a certain point, he realized that he couldn't keep living like this. It was simply too much to handle. That was the day that he decided to take the first step toward getting help for his anxiety.

As he walked into his new therapist's office, he could feel his heart beating in his throat. His hands were clamming up, and his anxiety was practically screaming at him to turn around and go back home — but he stayed. It took a minute for him to warm up to his therapist, but once he started talking about his thoughts and feelings, he realized that she wasn't there to judge him. She was actually listening to what he was saying, and trying to understand.

After just a few weeks of attending therapy, Charles began to feel better. His therapist told him about some coping strategies he could use to deal with his anxiety while at work or social gatherings. He learned that he wasn't alone in his struggles with anxiety and that seeking help is actually a sign of strength, not weakness. Of course, Charles's anxiety didn't disappear completely, but he had the tools to manage it now — which made him feel more safe and secure in all areas of his life.

He started talking to his girlfriend, friends, and family about his experiences with anxiety, and was surprised to find out that many of them struggled with anxiety as well. In the end, he was proud of himself for facing his anxiety head-on and getting the help he needed. He also hoped that his story would encourage other people in his position to seek help as well, which is why I've been sharing his story with you throughout this book.

In this chapter, we'll take a closer look at some of the main anxiety management strategies Charles learned about below. I encourage you to take some time to try out the techniques and exercises that speak to you

— especially if you're feeling anxious about an upcoming work presentation or social event. You might be surprised by how helpful the following anxiety management strategies can be. Who knows? Maybe you'll decide to integrate some of them into your daily routine. Let's dive right in, shall we?

## Relaxation Techniques

Have you ever had someone tell you to "just relax?" This can obviously be frustrating, especially for people with anxiety — who want, more than anything, to be able to relax! If you've ever experienced intense anxiety, you know that managing it isn't as simple as just relaxing. That's where relaxation techniques, like mindfulness meditation and progressive muscle relaxation, come in. These techniques are typically used in conjunction with other types of therapy, such as cognitive behavioral therapy and exposure therapy.

Relaxation techniques are meant to focus on the body and reduce anxiety symptoms like muscle tension. Practicing these techniques can help you slow down your breathing and heart rate, as well as quiet your racing thoughts. In addition to practicing these techniques, doing things you enjoy and spending time with the people you love most can also help you to feel more relaxed. Let's go over some of the best relaxation techniques I came across in my research below.

### Progressive Muscle Relaxation

I briefly touched on progressive muscle relaxation in the last chapter, but I'd like to take this opportunity to really get into the nitty-gritty of this particular relaxation technique. Progressive Muscle relaxation helps to counteract your body's natural response to stress, which is known as the fight-or-flight response. This response is necessary, as it can help you respond in a way that protects you when you find yourself in a dangerous situation. However, people who suffer from anxiety often find that their fight-or-flight response gets triggered too often, and by things that aren't actually dangerous at all.

When your fight-or-flight response gets activated, it can put a lot of stress on your body. This is why anxiety sufferers will oftentimes experience physical symptoms — like stiffness and muscle pain. Relaxation techniques, like progressive muscle relaxation, essentially have the opposite effect on your body. Practicing progressive muscle relaxation is meant to trigger your body's relaxation response, which reduces your heart rate and alleviates any bodily tension. Progressive muscle relaxation can also help people become more aware of how their mental and physical stress is affecting them emotionally. This sense of awareness may eventually help you let go of the anxious thoughts and feelings that come up in stressful situations.

### How to Practice Progressive Muscle Relaxation

In order to better understand how progressive muscle relaxation works, I recommend trying this quick exercise. Make a tight fist with one of your hands, and notice any tightness and tension in your fingers and forearm. Count to ten, then release your first and allow your hand to relax completely. You should notice a huge difference in tension, and feel much more relaxed than you did before.

This approach of systematically increasing and then releasing tension in different muscle groups throughout your body is the basis for progressive muscle relaxation. By creating tension in your body, noticing it, and then releasing that tension, you can effectively learn how to alleviate your stress and get rid of your anxious thoughts. If you'd like to practice some progressive muscle relaxation right now, I would suggest finding a comfortable place to sit or lie down where you won't get distracted. Feel free to close your eyes if that helps you relax, but it's not required for this exercise.

Start by taking three to five deep breaths. Make sure to inhale through your nose and exhale through your mouth. Tense up your feet and begin to work your way up your body, tensing and releasing each muscle group, including your legs, glutes, abdomen, back, hands, arms, shoulders, neck, and face. Hold each muscle group for a few breaths before slowly releasing the tension. I recommend repeating this process in any areas where you feel particularly tense. Finish up by taking a few more deep breaths, and take note of how much more relaxed you feel.

Keep in mind that progressive muscle relaxation takes practice, so don't be discouraged if you feel like it doesn't immediately get rid of your bodily tension. Nothing is instantaneous, especially when it comes to managing anxiety symptoms. Keep practicing every day, and you'll eventually see results. Remember to be patient with your mind and body! That's a big part of using relaxation techniques like this to cope with your anxiety.

### Mindfulness Meditation

Chances are, you've heard about mindfulness meditation. Perhaps your boss leads you and your coworkers in a mindfulness meditation exercise at the start of every work day (in which case, you have an awesome boss), or maybe you had a professor in college who ended every class with a mindfulness meditation exercise. As the name suggests, mindfulness meditation combines meditation with mindfulness — which involves being fully present in the moment and acknowledging your thoughts and feelings without judgment.

Mindfulness meditation can be done in a lot of different ways, but it usually involves deep breathing and being aware of your mind and body. You don't need to use essential oils or candles while meditating unless you want to (some people find that these things help them relax). All you need is a quiet and comfortable place to sit for a few minutes. Remember: it's very important that you approach mindfulness meditation with a non-judgmental attitude.

### How to Practice Mindfulness Meditation

At the beginning of your mindfulness meditation journey, you might find it difficult to sit quietly, especially if there are a lot of distracting things happening around you. This is actually a normal part of mindfulness practice. Again, mindfulness involves being aware of how sitting still can make your thoughts race — but not judging those thoughts. I recommend starting with short meditation sessions, and gradually increasing the duration of these sessions as you become more comfortable with the practice.

It's always a good idea to choose a quiet, distraction-free place to meditate. This might be a little difficult for people with pets or small children, but just do the best you can. Wear comfortable clothing and remove your jewelry, shoes, or anything else that could potentially distract you. The goal is to create a peaceful and comfortable environment. Feel free to use things like candles, calming music, and essential oils while you meditate, but again, these things aren't necessary.

Here's a 20-minute guided mindfulness meditation you can do when you're feeling especially anxious: To begin this mindfulness meditation practice, start with a quick check-in. This will help you to become more aware of your current mental and physical state. Once you've done this, slowly direct your attention to your breathing.

Next, recall a specific event where you experienced anxiety. Be mindful of how this experience made you feel. Don't judge the anxiety or try to push it away — just observe it as it is. Take note of any emotions that come up during this reflection. Keep in mind that if you don't experience strong emotions, it doesn't mean you're doing the meditation incorrectly. Everyone experiences different emotions while practicing mindfulness meditation, and there's no "right way" to feel during it.

As you become more mindful of your anxiety, it may bring forth deeper layers of memories, thoughts, feelings, and physical experiences. Allow yourself to observe these thoughts and feelings without judgment and simply notice them as they arise. When you're ready, you can gradually shift your focus back to your breathing. As you bring this meditation to a close, take a moment to congratulate yourself for practicing mindfulness and listening to your mind and body. Not a lot of people are able to take the initiative to check in with their anxiety, but getting into the practice of doing so is a huge step towards overcoming your anxiety issues.

## Yoga

Sometimes, when people start to experience feelings of anxiety or are going through particularly stressful times, they turn to yoga for relief. The beauty of yoga is that it meets you where you're at. Even practicing one or two poses for just a few minutes every day can have a pretty significant impact on you're well-being if you're open to it. The combination of focusing on your breathing and being present during each yoga pose can help quiet your negative thoughts and improve your mood. Yoga is also really good for your body and can release a lot of physical stress and tension.

To get the most out of practicing yoga, you should try to be mindful of the sensations moving throughout your body as you move through each pose. Allow yourself to feel and experience any emotions that happen to come up, but don't judge or criticize yourself for feeling a certain way or experiencing a certain thought. Practicing yoga is all about connecting with your body and living in the present moment.

If you find that your thoughts start to scatter during a yoga session, don't worry. This happens all the time, and it's best not to judge yourself for it. Gently refocus your attention back on your mat, and continue moving through your poses. Try to keep in mind that yoga is a journey, and the more you practice, the easier it'll become for you to focus on the present moment as well as release any anxious thoughts or emotions that may be weighing you down. Let's go over some yoga poses that you can try out on your own below.

### Yoga Poses

Yoga is a physical and spiritual practice that has been around for thousands of years. It's an excellent stress reliever, and it's been proven to improve flexibility and increase bodily strength as well. There are *a lot* of different yoga poses, and each one is uniquely beneficial in its own way. Listed below are a few poses you can try out if you're looking to not only reduce your anxiety symptoms but improve your health and well-being overall.

**The Channel-Cleaning Breath (Nadhi Shodhana)**

This is a breathing exercise that can help to calm down your mind and reduce your stress. It involves alternating nostrils while breathing in and out. Pretty simple, right? This practice is often done before starting a yoga session in order to help clear the mind and focus on the practice that's ahead.

**The Hero Pose (Virasana)**

The Hero pose is a seated pose that yoga experts say can help to improve circulation and digestion. It can also help to stretch out your ankles and your knees, so this might be a great pose for you to try out if you spend a lot of time sitting or standing.

**The Tree Pose (Vrikshasana)**

The Tree pose is a standing pose that can help to improve your balance and overall stability. It involves standing on one foot with the other foot placed on the thigh of whichever leg you're standing on. This pose can also help to strengthen your legs, hips, and core. This one may take some practice, so don't be discouraged if you fall over on your first try!

**The Extended Triangle (Utthita Trikonasana)**

You'll do this pose while standing as well. The Extended Triangle pose can help to strengthen your legs and core. It involves reaching one arm down to the ground while extending the other arm up toward the ceiling.

**The Standing Forward Bend (Padangusthasana)**

The Standing Forward Bend is a forward fold pose that can help you stretch out your hamstrings and lower back. It's an especially great pose for releasing tension and calming the mind, so I definitely recommend giving it a try.

**The Cat and Cow Poses (or Marjaryasana and Bitilasana, Respectively)**

These poses are quite similar, and they're often done together in order to warm up the spine and stretch out the neck, hips, and shoulders. Both of these poses involve alternating between arching your back and rounding it (much like a cat).

THE BRIDGE POSE (Setubandha)

The Bridge pose is a backbend type of pose that can help to strengthen your hips, core, and legs. It can also help to stretch out your chest, shoulders, and neck. This one feels great, but it definitely takes some practice.

## Breathing Exercises

Most of the time, breathing is something you do without really thinking about it. It's just a natural part of being alive! Some people who suffer from severe anxiety, however, have to think a bit more about their breathing. A lot of the symptoms that are associated with anxiety can cause a person with an anxiety disorder to breathe in a way that can lead to all sorts of physical and emotional problems. Oftentimes, your breathing is actually what causes uncomfortable anxiety symptoms, such as shortness of breath, and the reason for that is that your anxiety and stress are not allowing you to breathe properly.

Thankfully, there are plenty of great breathing exercises out there that can help you to more effectively regulate your breathing and cope with your anxiety. The exercises discussed below will teach you how to slow down your breathing in times of stress. The especially great thing about these exercises is that you can do them whenever and wherever you need to. Let's dive right in, shall we?

## Deep Breathing

Deep breathing is one of the most popular techniques people with anxiety use to calm down when they're feeling stressed out. It involves inhaling slowly and deeply, holding your breath for a few seconds, and then exhaling. Repeat this exercise several times until you're feeling nice and relaxed. This might take a few minutes, so be patient with yourself!

## The Quieting Response

The Quieting Response technique is another breathing exercise that can help to reduce your stress and anxiety as it literally activates your body's relaxation response. It involves breathing in deeply through your nose and then exhaling slowly through your mouth while making a "shh" sound. This technique helps slow down your heart rate and relax your muscles. I can't recommend it enough!

### Belly Breathing

Belly breathing (which is also known as diaphragmatic breathing) is an especially popular breathing exercise. It involves breathing deeply from your belly instead of from your chest. This technique has been proven to reduce stress by activating one's parasympathetic nervous system. To practice this exercise, place one hand on your belly and the other on your chest. From there, inhale slowly through your nose and exhale slowly through your mouth.

### Pursed Lips Breathing

Pursed lips breathing is a technique that can help you regulate your breathing and cut down on anxiety symptoms like shortness of breath. It involves inhaling through your nose and then exhaling slowly through your pursed lips (as if you're whistling). This technique helps to slow down your breathing and relax your muscles, so if you have muscle tension, it's definitely worth a try.

## Grounding Techniques

If you suffer from anxiety, you're undoubtedly familiar with the unpleasant physical symptoms that typically accompany an anxiety attack. Your heart rate increases, your mouth gets dry, and your body starts to shake. You might also experience cold sweats and a sense of panic that can be awfully overpowering despite it being irrational. People with anxiety disorders, such as PTSD, often become absorbed in thoughts of past traumas or future uncertainties, which can trigger their fight-or-flight response. As I've already discussed, this common response can make one's brain perceive something that's not threatening as threatening, which can cause your body to prepare for a potential attack.

Using grounding techniques is an excellent way to cope with anxiety attacks, so it's a shame they're not talked about more. Grounding techniques are techniques that can help distract you when you're dealing with anxiety or panic attack symptoms. These techniques can be physical or mental and they can help you focus on the present moment and your surroundings, rather than on your anxious thoughts. Basically, by using grounding techniques, you can significantly reduce the intensity of your fight-or-flight response and regain a sense of control over your body and mind. Let's take a look at some common grounding techniques below. I recommend using one or two of these techniques when you begin to feel a panic attack coming on.

### *Physical Grounding Techniques*

One of the most popular grounding techniques out there is the 5-4-3-2-1 technique. This technique involves naming five things you can see, four things you can touch, three things you can hear, two things you can smell, and one thing you can taste in order to distract yourself during a moment of panic. By focusing on these sensory experiences, you can shift your attention away from your anxious thoughts and emotions, and become more grounded in the moment — which, of course, is what truly matters.

Another way to ground yourself is by using certain physical sensations to sort of "trick" yourself and divert your attention away from your anxiety symptoms. For example, you can pour water over your hands, clench your fists and then release them, or wrap a heated blanket around your body. By paying attention to these sensations, you'll be able to calm yourself down and feel more at ease.

## *Mental Grounding Techniques*

MENTAL GROUNDING TECHNIQUES can also be quite helpful. For example, some people with anxiety will play memory games in their minds in order to distract themselves from their symptoms. Try to think in categories, use math and numbers, recite something, or make yourself laugh by reading a joke book or watching a funny video. These techniques can help shift your focus away from your anxiety and towards something a little healthier. You'll be able to give yourself a more structured and controlled mindset, and there's a lot of power in that.

## Segue

Coping with anxiety isn't easy, but with a little time and practice, it's totally possible. Now that you have the right information and tools on hand, you should be able to effectively soothe yourself when you're feeling anxious or stressed out. In the next chapter, I'll start to wrap things up and discuss some daily habits you can integrate into your routine if you want to live a less anxious life.

# 8

# DAILY HABITS FOR A LESS ANXIOUS LIFE

*"Whoever has learned to be anxious in the right way has learned the ultimate."*

— SØREN KIERKEGAARD

**E**very single one of us has habits — good and bad. Perhaps you've gotten into the habit of flossing daily, or maybe you chew your fingernails when you're feeling bored or stressed out. You've probably heard the phrase "old habits die hard." There's a lot of truth in that. It's *hard* to give up bad habits that you've been indulging in for a long time, but it's not impossible. The more you tell yourself that it's impossible, the harder it'll be to overcome anxious habits like isolating yourself from your friends or drinking too much as a way of coping with your anxiety.

When it comes to altering your habits and making lifestyle changes, it's important to start small. Although some bad habits — like smoking cigarettes — may be effectively overcome using the "cold turkey" method, social anxiety habits, such as refusing to go out with your friends, should be overcome by taking baby steps. It's easy for people with anxiety to get over-stimulated when too much is happening at once. Most anxious people carry a heavy fear of change around with them, which is why plunging yourself into the icy water might not be the best way to go about altering your lifestyle. Take your time, and inch yourself in. Eventually, you won't even notice how cold the water is.

Take this quote from Linda Esposito on Psychology Today: "You can read all the anti-anxiety advice in the world, but none of it matters unless you take action. To feel more relaxed, to sleep soundly at night, and to put energy into what matters, you have to stop wasting time on tasks that don't matter." In order to truly experience relief and achieve a more relaxed state of mind, you must take action and actively work towards reducing the stress and anxiety in your life. This might involve prioritizing tasks that are important to you and avoiding wasting time on activities that aren't actually benefiting you all that much.

By focusing on tasks that are meaningful and avoiding those that are not, you can channel your energy and attention toward the things that matter most. Keep in mind that you may need to set boundaries with certain people or give up activities that drain your energy if you want to change your lifestyle for the better. Soon enough, you'll be able to create a daily routine that supports your mental health and allows room for activities that truly bring you joy. Let's take a look at some anxiety-reducing habits that you can begin to integrate into your daily routine below. Follow these tips, and you'll be that much closer to taking your life back from anxiety.

## Get Some Sleep

I know that this is definitely easier said than done for people with anxiety, but just bear with me. If your anxiety has been keeping you from getting a good night's sleep, your lack of sleep has likely been making your anxiety worse. It's a vicious cycle. You can't sleep *because* of your anxiety, and your anxiety acts up *because* you can't sleep. Don't worry, though, because there are a few things you can do to break this cycle and finally get some shut-eye.

## *What to Do When You Can't Sleep*

One of the best things you can do is establish a consistent sleep routine. Try to go to bed at the same time every night and wake up at the same time every morning. Yes, this includes weekends! If you're having trouble falling asleep, try getting up and doing something relaxing — like taking a warm bath or watching an ASMR video — until you feel more sleepy. It may also be helpful to limit naps to less than an hour during the day.

You should also try to avoid caffeine (coffee, soda, etc), as caffeine can take up to eight hours to wear off. If you have panic attacks, it might be a good idea to avoid caffeine entirely. You should also review your medications with your doctor to see if any of your daily stimulants have been keeping you up at night.

Creating a comfortable sleep environment is also crucial. Keep your bedroom cool, dark, and quiet, and avoid using electronic devices like your phone or computer while in bed (unless you're listening to relaxing music or watching a relaxing video to help you sleep). If your mattress is uncomfortable, consider buying a new one. It'll be well worth the investment! If you're still having trouble falling asleep, try meditating or practicing deep breathing. Keep a sleep log to track your sleep patterns and monitor your progress. This will be a good way to determine whether or not the methods you've been trying are helping or not.

## Watch What You Eat

Did you know that maintaining a healthy diet is a crucial part of effectively managing anxiety? As delicious and comforting as pizza and soda may be, chances are, these unhealthy foods are negatively affecting your mental health. When it comes to eating healthy, there are a lot of dietary factors to consider. You should be hydrating properly, and getting enough complex carbohydrates (typically found in fruits and vegetables). It's also a good idea to avoid foods that are high in simple carbohydrates and to eat regularly to prevent your blood sugar from dropping too low.

### Anti-Anxiety Foods

Nobody is born knowing what to eat when it comes to maintaining a healthy diet and quelling anxiety symptoms. Listed below are some foods you should keep in mind the next time you take a trip to your local grocery store or farmer's market:

- Fatty fish
- Eggs
- Probiotics
- Pumpkin seeds
- Yogurt
- Green tea
- Asparagus
- Dark chocolate
- Turmeric
- Chamomile
- Brazil nuts
- Magnesium
- Antioxidant-rich foods (such as black beans, cherries, blueberries, apples, nuts, and leafy greens)
- Zinc
- Vitamin B

## Exercise

IF YOU'VE EVER FELT LESS STRESSED out after going for a run or working out with your friends at the gym, there's a good reason for it. To quote Elle Woods from *Legally Blonde* (2001): "Exercise gives you endorphins. Endorphins make you happy! Happy people don't shoot their husbands. They just don't!" Basically, when you take care of your body, you are taking care of your mind as well. It can be difficult to get into a daily exercise routine at first, but take it as slowly as you need to. Even just going for a nature walk for thirty minutes every other day is better than nothing.

## Detox From Social Media

If you're like most people, your relationship with social media has become a daily habit, and — whether you're aware of it or not — social media absolutely consumes your mental energy. We're constantly checking our phones for notifications, taking pictures for Instagram, and engaging in heated debates on Twitter and Facebook. Although social media can be fun, it's frankly gotten a little bit out of control. Thankfully, for people with anxiety, a social media detox can offer some much-needed relief.

It's important to remember that social media is not an accurate representation of real life. It presents a curated and selective view of the world, and people are beginning to recognize this fact. Consequently, there has been a growing trend of people reducing their social media usage, with some even deleting their accounts altogether. Social media, however, can be a harrowing addiction. While some people are able to quit cold turkey, many will quit for a short period of time and then go back to it. I think this is actually okay, though. Sometimes, people just need a break.

You don't need to go to extreme measures in order to reap the benefits of a social media detox. Simply taking a break from social media can help alleviate the anxiety that's associated with excessive social media use. So, instead of reaching for your phone first thing in the morning, I recommend trying to use your mental energy for more productive purposes. Go for a walk in nature, or curl up with your favorite book and a cup of coffee. By taking a step back from social media, you should be able to redirect your focus to the things that are truly important to you in life.

## Treat Yourself and Practice Self-Care

When you think about self-care, your mind might conjure up images of luxurious face masks, soothing massages, or an indulgent bubble bath with a glass of wine in hand. However, let's not forget that self-care doesn't have to be expensive or involve excessive pampering. In fact, some of the most impactful self-care practices are completely free and can transform your life if you learn how to integrate them into your daily routine. Self-care is a versatile term. It basically encompasses any sort of action we take that prioritizes our physical and mental health. This means that while we may associate self-care with spoiling ourselves, it's really just about taking care of ourselves in small and meaningful ways.

### Things You Can Do to Treat Yourself

Simple activities — such as stretching and dancing around the living room — can improve your mood and help you get into a more relaxed state of mind. Movement, in general, is a great way to release all of that tension and stress that's been building up over time. Doing little things for yourself, like making your bed in the morning or planning your dream vacation, can give you a boost of energy, as can practicing positive self-talk in the mirror or going for a walk in the park.

If you often feel stressed about things like work and house chores, writing an "it's done" list could be a great way to keep track of everything you have to do. It'll also make you feel more productive and accomplished, which is always nice. Taking short naps throughout the day or engaging in mindfulness meditation exercises are also excellent ways to practice self-care. I also recommend journaling fairly regularly, as that can be a great way to keep track of your thoughts as well as the progress you've been making with overcoming your anxiety.

Remember to celebrate the little things. Make a

special dinner for your significant other when the weekend finally rolls around, or treat yourself by doing absolutely nothing after you get home from work. You can also practice self-care while you're at work by taking frequent breaks, chatting with your coworkers, and going for little walks around the block every now and then. Do things that make you happy every single day, and your anxiety symptoms will lessen. It may take some time, but it will absolutely be worth it.

## Declutter

Life tends to build up, and sometimes, there's just way too much going on in your personal space. Clutter can be overwhelming for people with anxiety, so it's a good idea to declutter your space every once in a while. That said, it's important that you take it slow and start small. Begin by choosing just one small area in your home to organize — like a drawer or a shelf — and work on that until it's completely decluttered. The last thing you want to do is overwhelm yourself further by attempting to declutter everything at once.

Once you've cleared out the clutter from the space you're working on, consider categorizing your belongings into four different boxes, which you can mark "keep," "donate," "toss," or "sell." This should make the decluttering process a whole lot easier for you, and hey — it's a good excuse to have a yard sale.

Try to keep in mind that decluttering isn't a one-time event. It's an ongoing process, and it's certainly more of a marathon than it is a sprint. Decluttering can also extend beyond your physical things. Consider making your office space paperless, adding a "no junk mail" sign to your letterbox, and keeping track of the clothing you typically wear. These small changes can help you create a more minimalist, stress-free environment for yourself.

## Segue

Changing your lifestyle can be challenging, but if you're willing to take baby steps, you should eventually be able to alter your bad habits and reduce your anxiety. Getting more exercise, watching what you eat, and engaging in daily self-care activities are all excellent ways to quell your anxiety symptoms. Figure out what works best for you and keep at it. Although it might take a little bit of time, you're bound to see some significant improvements.

# CONCLUSION

Anxiety is one of the most commonly experienced mental illnesses in the world. It's honestly baffling that people don't talk about it more! The more you're able to understand your anxiety, the more success you'll have in eventually overcoming it (or, at the very least, learning how to manage it effectively). When it comes to coping with and overcoming your anxiety symptoms, one of the first things you're going to want to do is identify your triggers.

Some of the most common anxiety triggers include money problems, grief, illness, and job loss or work stress. In essence, big life changes can be difficult for people with anxiety to grapple with, as can significant past trauma — such as events that caused you emotional pain during your childhood or bad experiences you've had in past romantic relationships. Social anxiety can also be a huge problem, as it can negatively affect your relationships with your loved ones and prevent you from living your best life.

Thankfully, there are a whole lot of strategies and methods you can use to cope with your anxiety these days. Practicing things like mindfulness meditation and progressive muscle relaxation can have a significant impact on your mind and body, as well as reduce your anxiety symptoms (as long as you're willing to stick with it and practice every day). Some people with anxiety choose to take up yoga, which can really help with physical symptoms like muscle tension and stiffness. Practicing breathing exercises and engaging in grounding techniques can also help those who are experiencing a lot of anxiety all at once. These things tend to be especially helpful in the context of panic attacks.

By taking the actions required to slowly alter your habits, you can eventually change your life for the better. Getting daily exercise and keeping better track of what you eat can work wonders, as can getting more sleep and practicing self-care. Most people don't do enough things that bring them genuine joy in their daily lives, which is just one reason why anxiety is on the rise. It took my friend, Charles, a long time to learn this. However, when things clicked for him, he knew exactly how to take control of his anxiety and change his life.

Now that you have a lot more tools and information on hand, you should be able to take that first step toward overcoming your anxiety. I believe in you! As I mentioned before, this process won't be easy, but you'll be glad that you put the time and effort into taming the beast that's been holding you back from experiencing all of the joys life has to offer. Charles (and many others) eventually learned how to tame the beast with many faces, and you can too!

I hope that this book taught you something new, and helped you understand the complex nature of anxiety in a new light. Living with anxiety is *hard*, but you'll get through this — especially since you have a brand new tool belt. Keep building up your support system, and don't be afraid to seek professional help for your anxiety if you find yourself continuing to struggle with it. If you want to help other people who are struggling with anxiety, you can do so by leaving a review. Reviews from people like you are what will make this book more visible to those who are seeking help and solace while dealing with this common affliction.

You did it!

I would like to take a moment to express my deepest gratitude to you for taking the time to read this book on overcoming anxiety. I know that there are many books out there on this topic, and I am honored that you chose mine. I hope that you have found value in the pages of this book and that it has provided you with practical strategies and tools to manage your anxiety.

Writing this book was a labor of love, and it is my sincere hope that it has made a positive impact on your life. I know firsthand how challenging anxiety can be, and I wrote this book with the hope of helping others who are struggling with similar challenges. Whether you are dealing with everyday worries or more severe anxiety, my goal was to provide you with a roadmap for managing your anxiety and living a more fulfilling life.

As I bring this book to a close, I would like to ask for your help. If you found value in this book, **please consider leaving an honest review on Amazon**. Your feedback is invaluable and will help others who are considering purchasing this book. Your review will also let me know how I can improve future editions, and I am always open to feedback and suggestions.

Once again, thank you for reading this book on overcoming anxiety. Your support and encouragement mean the world to me, and I hope that this book has provided you with the tools you need to manage your anxiety and live a more fulfilling life.

Your Friend,

Kirk Teachout

# RESOURCES

*15 ways to improve your focus and concentration skills*. 15 Ways to Improve Your Focus and Concentration Skills. (n.d.). Retrieved March 9, 2023, from https://www.betterup.com/blog/15-ways-to-improve-your-focus-and-concentration-skills

Amy Morin, L. C. S. W. (2023, February 14). *Are you overthinking? here's how to tell*. Verywell Mind. Retrieved March 9, 2023, from https://www.verywellmind.com/how-to-know-when-youre-overthinking-5077069

Anna Katharina Schaffner, P. D. (2023, March 3). *Core beliefs: 12 worksheets to challenge negative beliefs*. PositivePsychology.com. Retrieved March 9, 2023, from https://positivepsychology.com/core-beliefs-worksheets

Barker, W. (2020, February 26). *The 9 emotional needs everyone has + how to meet them*. mindbodygreen. Retrieved March 9, 2023, from https://www.mindbodygreen.com/articles/9-emotional-needs-according-to-maslow-s-hierarchy

Becker, J. (2022, August 22). *The 10 most important things to simplify in your life*. Becoming Minimalist. Retrieved March 9, 2023, from https://www.becomingminimalist.com/the-10-most-important-things-to-simplify-in-your-life/

Buggy, P. (2020, May 19). *Fear setting: The step-by-step exercise Tim Ferriss uses to Conquer Fear*. Mindful Ambition. Retrieved March 9, 2023, from https://mindfulambition.net/fear-setting-tim-ferriss/

*Changing habits*. Learning Center. (2022, June 6). Retrieved March 9, 2023, from https://learningcenter.unc.edu/tips-and-tools/changing-habits/

Cherry, K. (2022, November 6). *Types of cognitive biases that distort how you think.* Verywell Mind. Retrieved March 9, 2023, from https:// www.verywellmind.com/cognitive-biases-distort-thinking-2794763

Cherry, K. (2022, November 7). *The fight-or-flight response prepares your body to take action.* Verywell Mind. Retrieved March 9, 2023, from https://www.verywellmind.com/what-is-the-fight-or-flight-response-2795194

Cherry, K. (n.d.). *Emotions and types of emotional responses.* Verywell Mind. Retrieved March 9, 2023, from https://www.verywellmind. com/what-are-emotions-2795178

Choksi, D. (2021, August 8). *Science explains overthinking.* Medium. Retrieved March 9, 2023, from https://medium.com/indian-thoughts/science-explains-overthinking-b709d0ec4dca

Council, F. C. (2022, October 12). *Council post: 13 ways to overcome negative thought patterns.* Forbes. Retrieved March 9, 2023, from https:// www.forbes.com/sites/forbescoachescouncil/2016/05/09/13-coaches-explain-how-to-overcome-negative-thought-patterns/

Edberg, H. (2022, June 10). *34 quotes to help you to stop overthinking (+ my 5 favorite tips).* The Positivity Blog. Retrieved March 9, 2023, from https://www.positivityblog.com/overthinking-quotes/

Eklof, K. (2020, June 18). *What happens to your body when you overthink?* Edexec. Retrieved March 9, 2023, from https://edexec.co.uk/what-happens-to-your-body-when-you-overthink/

Entefy. (2022, March 31). *How much information do you need to make smart decisions? - entefy: AI & Automation.* Entefy. Retrieved March 9, 2023, from https://www.entefy.com/blog/how-much-informa tion-do-you-need-to-make-smart-decisions/

*The Five steps to risk assessment explained.* Risk Assessor :: The five steps to risk assessment explained. (n.d.). Retrieved March 9, 2023, from https://www.riskassessor.net/news/detail/five-steps-to-risk-assessment

Garrett, L., Pratt, M., Hasenkamp, W., Goh, C., PhD, B. G. B., Kira M. Newman and Janet Ho, Newman, K. M., & Staff, M. (2023, January 6). *Getting started with mindfulness.* Mindful. Retrieved March 9,

2023, from https://www.mindful.org/meditation/mindfulness-getting-started/

Hanh, T. N. (2022, November 9). *Five steps to mindfulness*. Mindful. Retrieved March 9, 2023, from https://www.mindful.org/five-steps-to-mindfulness/

*How the parasympathetic nervous system can lower stress*. Hospital for Special Surgery. (n.d.). Retrieved March 9, 2023, from https://www.hss.edu/article_parasympathetic-nervous-system.asp

*How to deal with feeling emotionally overwhelmed - talkspace*. Mental Health Conditions. (2022, November 28). Retrieved March 9, 2023, from https://www.talkspace.com/mental-health/conditions/articles/feeling-overwhelmed/

Itani, O. (2022, December 27). *You are what you think: How your thoughts create your reality*. OMAR ITANI. Retrieved March 9, 2023, from https://www.omaritani.com/blog/what-you-think

Kinoshita T;Nagata S;Baba R;Kohmoto T;Iwagaki S; (n.d.). *Cold-water face immersion per se elicits cardiac parasympathetic activity*. Circulation journal : official journal of the Japanese Circulation Society. Retrieved March 9, 2023, from https://pubmed.ncbi.nlm.nih.gov/16723802/

Leo Newhouse, L. I. C. S. W. (2021, March 1). *Is crying good for you?* Harvard Health. Retrieved March 9, 2023, from https://www.health.harvard.edu/blog/is-crying-good-for-you-2021030122020#:

Maughan, T. (2020, November 30). *The modern world has finally become too complex for any of us to understand*. Medium. Retrieved March 9, 2023, from https://onezero.medium.com/the-modern-world-has-finally-become-too-complex-for-any-of-us-to-understand-1a0b46fbc292

MediLexicon International. (n.d.). *Core beliefs: Definition, how to identify, and more*. Medical News Today. Retrieved March 9, 2023, from https://www.medicalnewstoday.com/articles/core-beliefs

MediLexicon International. (n.d.). *What is diaphragmatic breathing? benefits and how-to*. Medical News Today. Retrieved March 9, 2023, from https://www.medicalnewstoday.com/articles/diaphragmatic-breathing

Moderndayomblog. (2021, August 19). *7 signs you're overthinking something as an HSP.* Sensitive Refuge. Retrieved March 9, 2023, from https://highlysensitiverefuge.com/7-signs-youre-overthinking-something-as-an-hsp/

MSW, W. by: I. W., & MD, R. by: K. F. (n.d.). *How to overcome your inner critic.* Choosing Therapy. Retrieved March 9, 2023, from https://www.choosingtherapy.com/overcome-inner-critic/

Raypole, C. (2020, April 28). *How to control your emotions: 11 strategies to try.* Healthline. Retrieved March 9, 2023, from https://www.health line.com/health/how-to-control-your-emotions

schneik4. (2022, December 9). *Overthinking disorder: Is it a mental illness?* Cleveland Clinic. Retrieved March 9, 2023, from https://health.clevelandclinic.org/is-overthinking-a-mental-illness/

Seeber, C. (2022, April 12). *Confessions of a recovering Overthinker.* Circle In. Retrieved March 9, 2023, from https://circlein.com/confessions-of-a-recovering-overthinker/

Seladi-Schulman, J. (2018, July 24). *What part of the brain controls emotions? fear, happiness, anger, Love.* Healthline. Retrieved March 9, 2023, from https://www.healthline.com/health/what-part-of-the-brain-controls-emotions

Sussex Publishers. (n.d.). *7 ways to get yourself unstuck.* Psychology Today. Retrieved March 9, 2023, from https://www.psychologyto day.com/za/blog/women-s-mental-health-matters/201612/7-ways-get-yourself-unstuck

*Thinking too much; and thinking too little.* The School Of Life. (n.d.). Retrieved March 9, 2023, from https://www.theschooloflife.com/article/thinking-too-much-and-thinking-too-little/

Visé, D. de. (2022, December 26). *More adult children are living with their parents. parents are not pleased.* The Hill. Retrieved March 9, 2023, from https://thehill.com/policy/finance/3777185-more-adult-children-are-living-with-their-parents-parents-are-not-pleased/

Walker, T. (n.d.). *14 mantras to repeat when things feel stressful.* Shine. Retrieved March 9, 2023, from https://advice.theshineapp.com/articles/mantras-to-repeat-when-things-feel-stressful/

*What is overthinking disorder?* BetterHelp. (n.d.). Retrieved March 9, 2023, from https://www.betterhelp.com/advice/personality-disorders/what-is-overthinking-disorder/

Wignall, N. (2021, February 17). *7 psychological reasons you overthink everything.* Nick Wignall. Retrieved March 9, 2023, from https://nickwignall.com/7-psychological-reasons-you-overthink-everything/

# RESOURCES

*10 easy ways to declutter your home: AIG Insurance Ireland.* aig. (n.d.). Retrieved April 13, 2023, from https://www.aig.ie/our-blog/ways-to-declutter-your-home

*9 common myths & facts about anxiety: Symptoms and treatment options.* The Recovery Village Drug and Alcohol Rehab. (2022, May 26). Retrieved April 13, 2023, from https://www.therecoveryvillage.com/mental-health/anxiety/anxiety-myths/

American Psychological Association. (n.d.). *Anxiety.* American Psychological Association. Retrieved April 13, 2023, from https://www.apa.org/topics/anxiety

*Anxiety disorders: Types, causes, symptoms & treatments.* Cleveland Clinic. (n.d.). Retrieved April 13, 2023, from https://my.cleveland clinic.org/health/diseases/9536-anxiety-disorders

Association, A. C. M. H. (n.d.). *What's the difference between anxiety and an anxiety disorder?* What's the difference between anxiety and an anxiety disorder? | Here to Help. Retrieved April 13, 2023, from https://www.heretohelp.bc.ca/q-and-a/whats-the-difference-between-anxiety-and-an-anxiety-disorder

Cronkleton, E. (2018, June 6). *Yoga for anxiety: 11 poses to try, why it works, and more.* Healthline. Retrieved April 13, 2023, from https://www.healthline.com/health/anxiety/yoga-for-anxiety

Cuncic, A. (2020, May 30). *Seek help for the worst triggers in social anxiety.* Verywell Mind. Retrieved April 13, 2023, from https://www.verywellmind.com/which-situations-trigger-anxiety-3024887

Dan. (2021, October 20). *25 grounding techniques for anxiety.* Choose Mental Health. Retrieved April 13, 2023, from https://choosemen talhealth.org/25-grounding-techniques-for-anxiety/

Dibdin, E. (2022, January 31). *When childhood trauma leads to anxiety.*

Psych Central. Retrieved April 13, 2023, from https://psychcentral. com/anxiety/the-connection-between-childhood-trauma-and-generalized-anxiety-disorder%23treatment-options

*Exercise for stress and anxiety.* Exercise for Stress and Anxiety | Anxiety and Depression Association of America, ADAA. (n.d.). Retrieved April 13, 2023, from https://adaa.org/living-with-anxiety/manag ing-anxiety/exercise-stress-and-anxiety

Forbes Magazine. (2023, March 9). *4 expert-backed breathing exercises for anxiety.* Forbes. Retrieved April 13, 2023, from https://www.forbes. com/health/mind/breathing-exercises-anxiety/

*Grief and anxiety.* Cruse Bereavement Support. (2021, November 15). Retrieved April 13, 2023, from https://www.cruse.org.uk/under standing-grief/effects-of-grief/grief-and-anxiety/

*How anxiety affects men and women differently.* How Anxiety Affects Men and Women Differently. (n.d.). Retrieved April 13, 2023, from https://www.texashealth.org/Health-and-Wellness/Behavioral-Health/How-Anxiety-Affects-Men-and-Women-Differently

Margarita Tartakovsky, M. S. (2017, November 20). *Why our family triggers USAND what to do.* Psych Central. Retrieved April 13, 2023, from https://psychcentral.com/blog/weightless/2017/11/why-our-family-triggers-us-and-what-to-do#1

Margarita Tartakovsky, M. S. (2021, September 14). *How to identify the real cause of your anxiety.* Psych Central. Retrieved April 13, 2023, from https://psychcentral.com/anxiety/getting-to-the-root-of-your-anxiety

Mayo Foundation for Medical Education and Research. (2020, March 11). *Obsessive-compulsive disorder (OCD).* Mayo Clinic. Retrieved April 13, 2023, from https://www.mayoclinic.org/diseases-condi tions/obsessive-compulsive-disorder/symptoms-causes/syc-20354432

Mayo Foundation for Medical Education and Research. (2022, December 13). *Post-traumatic stress disorder (PTSD).* Mayo Clinic. Retrieved April 13, 2023, from https://www.mayoclinic.org/

diseases-conditions/post-traumatic-stress-disorder/symptoms-causes/syc-20355967

Mcmaster, G. (2020, January 28). *Millennials and gen Z are more anxious than previous generations: Here's why.* Folio. Retrieved April 13, 2023, from https://www.ualberta.ca/folio/2020/01/millennials-and-gen-z-are-more-anxious-than-previous-generations-heres-why.html

MediLexicon International. (n.d.). *9 foods that help reduce anxiety.* Medical News Today. Retrieved April 13, 2023, from https://www.medicalnewstoday.com/articles/322652%23foods-that-help-reduce-anxiety

Melinda Smith, M. A. (2023, February 28). *Job loss and unemployment stress.* HelpGuide.org. Retrieved April 13, 2023, from https://www.helpguide.org/articles/stress/job-loss-and-unemployment-stress.htm

Migdol, E. (2023, February 28). *10 conditions that may be misdiagnosed as anxiety.* The Mighty. Retrieved April 13, 2023, from https://themighty.com/topic/chronic-illness/misdiagnosed-anxiety-symptoms/

Miller, H. A. (2020, July 14). *7 lesser known symptoms of anxiety.* Family Psychiatry & Therapy. Retrieved April 13, 2023, from https://familypsychnj.com/2020/07/7-lesser-known-symptoms-of-anxiety/

Murphy, A. (2022, July 4). *How to take a social media detox and improve your mental health.* Declutter The Mind. Retrieved April 13, 2023, from https://declutterthemind.com/blog/social-media-detox/

NHS. (n.d.). *NHS choices.* Retrieved April 13, 2023, from https://www.nhs.uk/mental-health/conditions/generalised-anxiety-disorder/symptoms/

Nicole J. LeBlanc, M. A., & Luana Marques, P. D. (2019, August 27). *Anxiety in college: What we know and how to Cope.* Harvard Health. Retrieved April 13, 2023, from https://www.health.harvard.edu/blog/anxiety-in-college-what-we-know-and-how-to-cope-2019052816729

*Postpartum anxiety: Causes, symptoms, diagnosis & treatment.* Cleveland

Clinic. (n.d.). Retrieved April 13, 2023, from https://my.cleveland clinic.org/health/diseases/22693-postpartum-anxiety

Robinson, L. (2023, February 25). *Coping with financial stress.* Help-Guide.org. Retrieved April 13, 2023, from https://www.helpguide. org/articles/stress/coping-with-financial-stress.htm

Robinson, L. (2023, March 4). *Coping with a life-threatening illness or serious health event.* HelpGuide.org. Retrieved April 13, 2023, from https://www.helpguide.org/articles/grief/coping-with-a-life-threat ening-illness.htm

*Social anxiety disorder.* Social Anxiety Disorder | Anxiety and Depression Association of America, ADAA. (n.d.). Retrieved April 13, 2023, from https://adaa.org/understanding-anxiety/social-anxiety-disorder

Sussex Publishers. (n.d.). *Getting past the past jealousy.* Psychology Today. Retrieved April 13, 2023, from https://www.psychologytoday. com/us/blog/anxiety-files/201804/getting-past-the-past-jealousy

Team, T. H. E. (2021, October 11). *What causes anxiety? risk factors and more.* Healthline. Retrieved April 13, 2023, from https://www.health line.com/health/anxiety-causes%23causes

*Tips for beating anxiety to get a better night's sleep.* Harvard Health. (2020, October 13). Retrieved April 13, 2023, from https://www. health.harvard.edu/mind-and-mood/tips-for-beating-anxiety-to-get-a-better-nights-sleep

Toussaint, L., Nguyen, Q. A., Roettger, C., Dixon, K., Offenbächer, M., Kohls, N., Hirsch, J., & Sirois, F. (2021, July 2). *Effectiveness of progressive muscle relaxation, deep breathing, and guided imagery in promoting psychological and physiological states of relaxation.* Evidence-based complementary and alternative medicine : eCAM. Retrieved April 13, 2023, from https://www.ncbi.nlm.nih. gov/pmc/articles/PMC8272667/

WebMD. (n.d.). *Workplace anxiety: Causes, symptoms, and treatment.* WebMD. Retrieved April 13, 2023, from https://www.webmd.com/ anxiety-panic/features/workplace-anxiety

*What are anxiety disorders?* Psychiatry.org - What are Anxiety Disorders? (n.d.). Retrieved April 13, 2023, from https://www.psychiatry.org/patients-families/anxiety-disorders/what-are-anxiety-disorders

*What lifestyle changes are recommended for anxiety and depression?* Taking Charge of Your Health & Wellbeing. (n.d.). Retrieved April 13, 2023, from https://www.takingcharge.csh.umn.edu/what-lifestyle-changes-are-recommended-anxiety-and-depression

Wolff, C. (2018, January 10). *21 quick, life-changing self-care hacks that don't cost you anything.* Bustle. Retrieved April 13, 2023, from https://www.bustle.com/p/21-quick-life-changing-self-care-hacks-that-dont-cost-you-anything-7842786

Printed in Great Britain
by Amazon

27907929R00198